POLITICAL PHILOSOPHY

PRINCETON FOUNDATIONS OF
CONTEMPORARY PHILOSOPHY

Scott Soames, Series Editor

Political Philosophy

THE PUZZLE OF
LEGITIMATE INJUSTICE

JONATHAN QUONG

PRINCETON UNIVERSITY PRESS

PRINCETON & OXFORD

Published by Princeton University Press
41 William Street, Princeton, New Jersey 08540
99 Banbury Road, Oxford OX2 6JX

press.princeton.edu

GPSR Authorized Representative: Easy Access System Europe - Mustamäe tee 50, 10621 Tallinn, Estonia, gpsr.requests@easproject.com

All Rights Reserved
ISBN 9780691215648
ISBN (e-book) 9780691279855

Library of Congress Control Number: 2025938087

British Library Cataloging-in-Publication Data is available

Editorial: Rob Tempio and Chloe Coy
Production Editorial: Sara Lerner
Jacket Design: Wanda España
Production: Erin Suydam
Publicity: William Pagdatoon
Copyeditor: Francis Eaves

This book has been composed in Arno

Printed in the United States of America

10 9 8 7 6 5 4 3 2 1

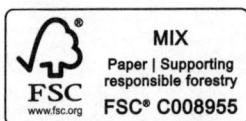

For Kira, Elia, and Hanna

CONTENTS

ACKNOWLEDGMENTS

I WOULD like to begin by thanking Scott Soames and Rob Tempio. In their roles as editors, they generously afforded me the latitude to write the sort of book about political philosophy that I wanted to write, and which I hope will be illuminating and useful for both specialists and non-specialists. I'm also very grateful for their patience as I, predictably, failed to meet several self-imposed deadlines.

I have been thinking about the issues covered in this book for a long time, and I have given talks about these ideas at many different venues. As a consequence, a lot of people have helped improve my thinking about these issues, both in conversation and with detailed written comments. I am thankful to the audiences at all the workshops, colloquia, and conferences where some of this work was initially presented. What follows is surely an incomplete list of people to whom I am very grateful for help: Emad Atiq, Christian Barry, Saba Bazargan-Forward, Chuck Beitz, Juliana Bidadanure, Joseph Bowen, Brookes Brown, David Clark, Garrett Cullity, Ryan Davis, Dave Estlund, Cécile Fabre, Helen Frowe, Paul Garofalo, Jerry Gaus, Bob Goodin, Jason Hanna, Debbie Hellman, Sean Ingham, Frank Jackson, Renée Jorgensen, Matt Kramer, Cécile Laborde, Gerald Lang, R. J. Leland, Andrew Lister, Andrei Marmor, Peter de Marneffe, Simon May, Liam Murphy, Mike Otsuka, Japa Pallikkathayil, Avia Pasternak, Alan Patten, Philip Pettit, Ryan Pevnick, Massimo Renzo, Gina Schouten, Mark Schroeder, Micah Schwartzman, Tom Sinclair, Nicholas Southwood, Hillel Steiner, Zosia Stemplowska, Annie

Stilz, Becca Stone, Adam Swift, Collis Tahzib, Rosa Terlazzo, Jean Thomas, Chad Van Schoelandt, Bas van der Vossen, Daniel Vie-hoff, Steve Wall, Paul Weithman, Kit Wellman, Leif Wenar, David Wiens, Yuan Yuan, Annette Zimmerman, and all those who participated in two different graduate seminars on the topic of legitimate injustice that I taught at the University of Southern California.

There are a few people from this list who have helped me so much that there is no way to adequately convey my gratitude. I have been talking about legitimate injustice with Tom Sinclair, with Zosia Stemplowska, and with Daniel Viehoff for many years. I've learned more about this topic from them than from anyone else, and their own exemplary work on legitimate injustice has been an important source of inspiration and motivation for me. Daniel also provided me with a huge amount of useful feedback on the penultimate version of the manuscript. Finally, as always, Becca is the person who has helped me the most. I am very sure that I don't deserve all this help from these exceptional people, but luckily for me, I get to have it anyway.

POLITICAL PHILOSOPHY

1

A Puzzle About Politics

SOME AREAS OF contemporary analytic philosophy have been dominated by a central question or debate: What is law? Are there mind-independent moral truths? What is knowledge? Contemporary political philosophy does not revolve around a single, central question in this way. That said, two questions have shaped the recent literature more than any of the others. These are, as Jonathan Wolff pithily presents them, "Who gets what?"; and "Says who?"[1]

The first is the question of social or distributive justice. Social life involves many benefits and burdens and we need principles that determine how those benefits and burdens should be allocated. How should entitlements to physical resources such as land be allocated? What principles should regulate the allocation of income and wealth? Most of us want to be free from the interference of others to pursue various activities, but how is the scope of this freedom determined, and what should we do when one person's apparent freedoms come into conflict with those of another? These are questions about what constitutes each person's rightful share of freedom, resources, and other advantages.

The second is the question of political legitimacy. Who has the authority to make rules regulating our shared social life and enforce compliance with those rules? Is this authority something

1. Wolff, *Introduction to Political Philosophy*, 1.

that we must share on an equal basis? Are individuals obligated to comply with the decisions made by a political authority, and if so, on what basis? What limits, if any, are there on the rightful authority of political institutions to issue and enforce laws?

These two general topics—justice and legitimacy—are often treated as distinct. It is common practice for political philosophers to develop and defend particular accounts of distributive justice without saying anything about what their theories imply for political legitimacy. Similarly, many accounts of political legitimacy or political obligation make few, if any, detailed claims about what justice requires. Someone surveying the literature from the last several decades might conclude that the truth about distributive justice doesn't depend much, if at all, on the truth about political legitimacy, and vice versa.

But this conclusion would be a mistake. When we look more closely, the concepts of justice and political legitimacy are deeply intertwined. Most of us believe, for example, that justice sets at least some substantive constraints on what a government may legitimately do. No government, for example, has the legitimate authority to sell citizens into slavery, or to force citizens to become members of a particular religious group. A theory of political legitimacy that countenanced such grave injustices would be false. Similarly, our considered convictions about justice are not independent of our views about legitimacy. Many of us believe, for example that it would be unjust—a violation of individual rights—for a benevolent dictator to impose the truth about justice on citizens who had democratically selected alternative rulers.

Justice and political legitimacy are the two most widely discussed concepts in contemporary political philosophy, and yet there is very little agreement—indeed surprisingly little direct work—about the way these concepts are related to each other. Although it's easy to point to examples where most of us agree that the truth about one concept partly determines the truth about the other, it is far from clear how to explain systematically the connection between the two concepts. A central project in political philosophy must be to correctly understand the relationship between justice and legitimacy.

To get a better grip on how puzzling and difficult it is to theorize the relationship between these two concepts, consider the following three claims:

1) "Justice is the first virtue of social institutions, as truth is of systems of thought. A theory however elegant and economical must be rejected or revised if it is untrue; likewise laws and institutions no matter how efficient and well-arranged must be reformed or abolished if they are unjust."[2]

2) Some ordinary laws in liberal democratic societies are unjust.

3) Many of these laws can be legitimate: that is, state officials act permissibly in enforcing these laws and they have rights against harmful interference while enforcing them.

Each claim, taken on its own, seems plausible. But the three claims are collectively in tension. If justice is the first virtue of social institutions and some ordinary laws are unjust, then it should not be permissible for state officials to impose these laws. Alternatively, if it is legitimate to impose unjust laws, then justice cannot be the first virtue of social institutions. Or, another alternative: if justice is the first virtue of social institutions and it is legitimate for state officials to impose all these laws, then we ought to conclude that these laws are not in fact unjust.

Many of us believe that there can be laws that are unjust and yet that these laws can be legitimately imposed. But how can this be true if, as many of us also believe, justice is the first virtue of social institutions? This is *the puzzle of legitimate injustice*.

This puzzle is deep and important. Surprisingly, however, it has not received much direct attention. No one, to my knowledge, has formulated it as an apparent trilemma in this way. And yet a great

2. Rawls, *Theory of Justice*, 3.

deal of recent work in political philosophy can be usefully understood as offering different frameworks that promise to dissolve the
puzzle in one way or another.

My primary aim in this book is to use the puzzle of legitimate
injustice as a vehicle for analyzing some recent, influential, work in
political philosophy. Doing so, I hope, is a novel and illuminating
way to learn about, and evaluate, some important views in the
field. But, to avoid any misunderstanding, this book is not a neutral survey of the literature. I will argue that leading accounts of
political morality lack an adequate solution to the puzzle. Moreover, the failures of these accounts to solve this puzzle are serious
and provide compelling reasons to revise or reject them. In the
book's final chapter, I offer my own view about how we ought to
address the puzzle, and I explain what this implies for more general theories of political morality.

Legitimate Injustice

In 1998 Tony Blair's Labour government introduced means-
tested tuition fees for students attending university in the United
Kingdom. The fee cap, initially set at £1,000, had multiplied to
£9,000 by 2012. Many opponents of these tuition fees argued that
such charges were unfair and unjust—in particular, that they
were disproportionately likely to deter already economically dis-
advantaged people from pursuing a university education. But,
as far as I am aware, these critics did not argue that, because
the policy was unjust, the British government would be acting
illegitimately.

In 2021, President Biden proposed raising the federal corporate
tax rate in the United States from 21 percent to 28 percent. The
Biden administration also proposed increasing the top individual
income tax rate from 37 percent to 39.6 percent and furthermore
applying the 12.4 percent payroll tax to all income above $400,000
per year. These proposals were presented by the administration as
a way of reducing economic inequality and ensuring tax burdens

were more equitably distributed between wealthy and less wealthy Americans. Some opponents argued that these increases were "outrageous" and "unjust."[3] But, to the best of my knowledge, these same opponents did not claim that, because they were unjust, the tax increases would be illegitimate. These are just two examples, but it would not be difficult to provide many, many more. In such cases, there is a sharp dispute about whether a proposed law is just. But those who allege the proposed law is unjust do not claim that the law would be illegitimate if enacted via the appropriate procedures.[4]

The view that laws can sometimes be unjust and yet legitimate is, I think, widely accepted by both laypersons and political philosophers. Here is G. A. Cohen articulating the thought: "Suppose that a democracy enacts a (not too) unjust law. I thought it was unjust when I voted against it, but I think that the state may now rightly impose it."[5] And here is John Rawls expressing roughly the same idea: "neither the [legitimate] procedures nor the laws need be just by a strict standard of justice, even if, what is also true, they cannot be too gravely unjust. [. . .] [L]aws cannot be too unjust if they are to be legitimate."[6] As both Cohen and Rawls emphasize, the idea is not that laws can be legitimate no matter how unjust. The more modest thought is simply that we cannot infer that a law is illegitimate because it is

3. See Leonhardt, "Biden's Modest Tax Plan"; and Stoll, "Here's How Biden's Proposed Tax Increases Will Affect You."
4. Throughout the book I use the terms "law" and "laws" in a positivist sense: that is, to refer to directives enacted via the constitutionally approved or widely accepted legal mechanisms in a jurisdiction. But the puzzle of legitimate injustice does not depend on adopting a version of legal positivism. The puzzle can also arise for theories of natural law insofar as they allow positive enactments sometimes to influence the content of law (e.g., a theory of natural law that merely holds that positive directives must meet certain minimal moral standards to count as law).
5. Cohen, "Fairness and Legitimacy," 7.
6. Rawls, Political Liberalism, 428–29.

unjust; some degree of injustice is consistent with a law being legitimate.

With this idea in hand, let's try to make the puzzle of legitimate injustice clearer by looking more closely at each of the three claims that generate the puzzle.

The Priority of Justice

Principles or theories of justice tell us how freedoms, resources, or other advantages ought to be allocated amongst persons; they purport to tell us what each person is entitled to as a matter of right. When someone is denied something to which she is entitled as a matter of justice she has typically been wronged; her rights have been infringed, or violated. Under at least a wide range of circumstances, we may permissibly use some force to defend such rights, or at least we may call upon the state to use its legal and coercive powers to defend such rights. When we are treated unjustly, we are also frequently entitled to compensation. Civil rights—for example, rights to freedom of speech, religion, and assembly—are paradigmatic claims of justice.

Justice, Rawls tells us, is the first virtue of social institutions. By that he means that it has lexical priority over other considerations when it comes to the design and implementation of our major political, legal, and economic institutions. This claim is, at least initially, intuitive. Almost everyone accepts, at least as an aspirational ideal, that our major social institutions should be just rather than unjust. Imagine someone proposing a constitutional amendment, or a modification to the existing legal regime, saying, "Yes, it's true that my proposal is unjust, but I favor the proposed change because it will achieve X." There's a reason people don't advance arguments of this kind. Such an argument would likely be dismissed as a kind misunderstanding of what our political and legal institutions are supposed to do. These institutions may have a plurality of functions, but whatever else they do, they must not be unjust; they must not deprive people of their civil liberties, or their other rightful entitlements.[7]

Still, the idea that justice should have lexical priority might sound unreasonably fanatical. In many contexts, it's more natural to consider trade-offs between values or considerations. When deciding where to live, we might trade the length of the commute off against the attractions of the local neighborhood. When designing a new transportation infrastructure for our city, we balance the cost against improved safety features. In these decisions—and so many others—it would be odd to identify one consideration as taking lexical priority over all the others. You wouldn't prioritize reducing your commute at any cost, nor would you prioritize safety features for the infrastructure plan no matter what the cost. So why take seriously the idea that justice has lexical priority for the basic structure of our political societies? The idea that justice has lexical priority is more plausible, however, once we understand the limited nature of the claim.[8]

First, the claim is not that substantive justice must be pursued without regard for procedural or democratic constraints. The claim is rather that unjust laws and policies must be reformed or abolished; but this is compatible with holding that reforming or abolishing unjust laws must be done via certain procedures— indeed, those procedural constraints may themselves be among the requirements of justice.[9]

7. Note that even if one denies that justice is the first virtue of social institutions in the sense described in this paragraph, one can still coherently affirm the idea that it is typically wrong for non-state actors to act unjustly, and that those who are threatened with rights violations typically are permitted to use force to defend their rights and are typically entitled to compensation when their rights are infringed.

8. Also note that the tension between our three claims is lessened, but clearly persists, if the first claim is weakened. Even if justice does not have lexical priority, so long as it is a very important virtue, or a normally decisive virtue, the existence of legitimate injustice remains puzzling.

9. If some procedural constraints are part of the content of justice, doesn't this easily or quickly dissolve the puzzle of legitimate injustice? We have an apparent

Second, the subject of the claim is restricted to the major political, legal, and economic institutions of a society: what Rawls calls the "basic structure."[10] When we are designing, creating, building, reforming, or abolishing these institutions or any of their constituent parts, considerations of justice take lexical priority. Even if these institutions serve other goals or can be aptly assessed according to other criteria, these other goals or criteria never take precedence over considerations of justice. We cannot, for example, restructure the constitution to deprive some citizens of their civil liberties, even if doing so would facilitate economic growth or help to sustain important religious or cultural practices. We can countenance unjust laws or institutions, Rawls says, "only when it is necessary to avoid an even greater injustice."[11]

Because the priority claim is limited to the basic structure, we can set aside certain worries. The priority of justice does not entail that individual persons have to grant justice lexical priority in their everyday decisions. For example, it doesn't necessarily follow that justice has lexical priority for individuals making choices about how to spend their leisure time or which career to pursue.[12] Another example: suppose justice demands certain important changes to the basic structure in order to combat climate change. The priority claim doesn't entail that you must accord lexical

explanation as to why substantively unjust decisions can be legitimate: they are the results of decision-procedures required by justice. But even if we stipulate that the content of justice includes some procedural requirements, it's not at all obvious why substantively unjust laws are legitimate. After all, why should the procedural requirements of justice reliably trump the substantive requirements of justice? As we will see in some of the chapters to follow (particularly chapter 5), some have tried to defend versions of this solution, but I argue that extant versions of the solution are unsuccessful.

10. Rawls, *Political Liberalism*, lecture VII.

11. Rawls, *Theory of Justice*, 4.

12. Even G. A. Cohen, who is otherwise skeptical of the distinction between personal choices and the basic structure, accepts that justice does not have lexical priority in many personal economic decisions. See Cohen, *Rescuing Justice and Equality*, 60–62.

priority to reducing your carbon emissions in all aspects of your personal life. This defuses, at least in part, worries that the priority claim poses an undue threat to personal integrity. People need not regard their lives as mere vehicles for securing or promoting justice, even if we insist that our major social institutions must be designed in a way that accords justice lexical priority.

Third, the scope of the priority claim is limited to reasonably favorable conditions. Conditions are reasonably favorable when "historical, economic and social conditions [. . . are] such that, provided the political will exists, effective political institutions can be established," that secure for each person their just share of freedom, resources, and other advantages.[13] Perhaps the most important feature of reasonably favorable conditions is moderate scarcity. Moderate scarcity entails there being resources that can be allocated amongst persons, and that while each person would prefer to have a greater rather than a lesser share, a just distribution of the resources remains possible. When there is extreme scarcity, by contrast, it becomes impossible to provide each person with his or her just share. A paradigm case of extreme scarcity is the overcrowded life raft: there are too many people aboard and so the life raft will sink, killing everyone, unless a minority are removed and left to die. It's not possible to create policies that secure for each person a fair share of the valuable resource (space on the raft). Under such conditions, the priority claim doesn't apply.[14] This limitation on scope defuses another worry: namely, that the priority claim commits us to ignoring consequentialist or lesser-evil justifications when we face emergency conditions or terrible shortages.

Finally, the priority claim must not be confused with a very different idea: the view that a duty to obey the laws of a legitimate

13. Rawls, *Justice as Fairness*, 47. In the quoted passage Rawls focuses more narrowly on the conditions needed to secure each person's basic rights and liberties. My definition of reasonably favorable conditions is more expansive.

14. I do not say that claims of justice do not exist in conditions of extreme scarcity; the point here is merely that the priority of justice may not obtain under those conditions.

state has priority over all other obligations or considerations. What the law requires and what justice requires can come apart—indeed this is among the central assumptions that generate the puzzle of legitimate injustice.

With those potential worries about the priority claim defused, it's easier to see why the claim is so appealing. Suppose that we confront reasonably favorable conditions whereby it's possible to design political institutions that allocate to each person his or her just share of freedom and other resources. Surely we must do this. We cannot decide to create or sustain unjust institutions instead. The most obvious reasons to accept some degree of injustice—averting great evils (e.g., where everyone on the life raft drowns) or concerns about individual demandingness or integrity—are off the table. What else could plausibly outweigh the importance of securing just institutions?

Many of the values or relationships that are commonly identified as important—family, friendship, communal belonging, moral virtue, intellectual excellence, artistic achievement—do not seem plausible candidates for at least two reasons. First, many of these considerations don't plausibly trump considerations of justice. I'm not aware of anyone who argues that it would be permissible or legitimate to violate individual moral rights to ensure greater forms of artistic achievement or intellectual excellence in our society, or to promote greater degrees of communal belonging.

Second, in a just society—one where everyone's rights are respected and each person has rightful entitlements to a fair share of resource or advantages—people can form happy families, forge deep and meaningful friendships, develop close communal associations, create great intellectual and artistic works, and so on. Indeed, we might insist that just institutions must facilitate and make possible valuable forms of life. As Rawls says,

> [S]urely just institutions and the political virtues expected of citizens would not be institutions and virtues of a just and good society unless those institutions and virtues not only permitted

but also sustained ways of life fully worthy of citizens' devoted allegiance. A political conception of justice must contain within itself sufficient space, as it were, for such ways of life. Thus, while justice draws the limit, and the good shows the point, justice cannot draw the limit too narrowly.[15]

It might, of course, be the case that certain values or achievements cannot be *maximized* within a just basic structure. Maybe slave labor is needed to realize the greatest possible intellectual or artistic achievement. But I'm not aware of any contemporary philosopher who argues that facts like these would constitute compelling reasons to reject the priority of justice.

Some might resist the priority claim because they hold that there are deep truths about morality or the good life—truths about what we owe to others or how we ought to live—and these truths take priority over anything else. Adherents of particular religions, for example, believe that God has provided specific instructions about how we must conduct ourselves. Since nothing can trump God's commands, justice cannot have lexical priority with regard to the basic structure of our society. Let's call this *the deep truths challenge* to the priority claim.

This challenge to the priority claim requires some unpacking. To begin, note what the challenge assumes: it assumes that the deep truths about morality or the good life are not included in the content of justice, or if they are included, are not accorded lexically prime status relative to other principles. One simple way to defuse the challenge is thus to reject this assumption—to stipulate that the correct theory of justice is congruent with all the deep truths about morality and the good life.

This solution, however, isn't available to most of the leading contemporary theories of justice. John Rawls, Robert Nozick, Ronald Dworkin, Michael Walzer, Iris Marion Young, G. A. Cohen, Elizabeth Anderson, and Martha Nussbaum (to name

15. Rawls, *Political Liberalism*, 174.

only some) have each presented theories of justice which explicitly do not purport to include all the deep truths there might be about morality or the good life. Put differently, contemporary theories of justice are virtually all limited in scope. They don't provide directives with regard to all aspects of our lives. They don't tell us how to worship, whom to marry, or what activities add value to the quality of our lives. Theories of justice are typically restricted to questions about the allocation of our civil and political liberties, the distribution of valuable opportunities (e.g., employment or education), and the distribution of income, wealth, welfare, or other valuable resources. Of course, to answer these questions, some theories do depend on deeper claims about what constitutes a good life, or what our wider ethical obligations to others look like. But even theories of justice that do so depend—and not all of them do—typically don't invoke the *whole* truth about morality, religion, or the good life. Their scope is limited to the rules and institutions required to ensure each person gets his or her fair or rightful share of social advantages. Contemporary theorists of justice are virtually united in assuming that we can answer this question about the rightful allocation of shares without specifying which religion is true, whether and how you should choose whom to marry, or which activities would most enrich your life. These theories thus cannot defuse the deep truths challenge by stipulating that the content of justice is congruent with all the deep truths about morality or the good life.

A different response to the challenge is to insist that theories of justice are designed to provide at least a partial solution to the fact that there is intractable disagreement about the deep truths of morality, religion, and the good life. We will never agree on which religion is true, or what activities and virtues most enrich a human life. It's partly because we can't agree on these issues that we require principles of justice to allocate to each person their fair share of freedom and other resources. By doing this, principles of justice provide each person with a rightful sphere within which we each pursue our own views about morality, religion, and the good life. Principles of justice effectively privatize some of our deepest disagreements, enabling us to live peacefully and cooperatively on fair terms with those with whom we sharply disagree.

We will explore different versions of this response in some of the chapters to follow. But for now, it's important to note that this response requires some controversial assumptions. It assumes that living peacefully and cooperatively with others on fair terms takes precedence over trying to structure our social institutions in accordance with the whole truth about morality, religion, or the good life. This response also assumes that what constitutes fair terms of cooperative life can be determined without appeal to the whole truth about morality, religion, or the good life.[16]

I have been canvassing and defusing various reasons to worry about the lexical priority claim. But I want to conclude this section by re-emphasizing how compelling and widely accepted the idea is. It's almost impossible to find anyone who seriously advances the view that we should give priority to considerations other than justice when determining what people's basic legal rights should be, or that our economic system should be rendered more unjust in order to better realize some other values. It's widely accepted that the prime function of our major political, legal, and economic rules and institutions is to establish just terms on which persons can interact. These rules and institutions purport to govern us— they claim the moral authority to regulate vast aspects of our lives. It is unclear why people would accept this authority unless these rules and institutions are at least constrained by the requirements of justice and individual moral rights.

Unjust Laws

The second claim that forms the puzzle of legitimate injustice is that some ordinary laws in liberal democratic societies are unjust. This idea is familiar and easy to grasp. Consider the two

16. This assumption, though controversial, is still more modest than the Rawlsian idea that fair terms of social cooperation can be determined without appeal to *any* reasonably disputed claims about morality, religion, or the good life, apart from a very thin notion of the good of free and equal citizens.

examples presented earlier: university tuition fees in the United Kingdom, and President Biden's proposed tax increases in the United States. In each case, many who opposed the government's proposals did so because they believed the proposals were unjust; they held that these proposals unjustly deprived lower-income students of a fair opportunity for a university education or that Biden's tax plan unjustly threatened financial freedoms. In any liberal democratic society there are constant disagreements about whether existing or proposed laws are just. Mask mandates during the COVID pandemic, the Affordable Care Act in the United States, laws restricting women's access to abortion, laws tying the funding of public schools to the property tax base of local communities, laws criminalizing prostitution, and the criminalization of recreational drug use are just a handful of further examples where critics have forcefully argued that proposed or enacted laws are unjust.

Indeed, despite increasing degrees of political polarization in some liberal democracies, one of the few truths about politics that most people would accept is this: all existing liberal democracies are, to some extent, unjust. Which laws in particular are unjust is, of course, a matter of sharp dispute, but the bare idea that at least some existing laws are unjust is not controversial. Given pervasive political disagreement, the fact that at least some ordinary laws are unjust is utterly unsurprising. We don't agree about what justice requires, and we can't all be correct. Unless one holds a very implausible view about the infallibility of majorities or the representatives that they elect, we should expect democracies to make mistakes; they will sometimes, maybe quite often, enact unjust legislation.

To be a bit more precise, the claim is not simply that, as a matter of historical record, some liberal democracies have enacted unjust laws. The claim is rather that some ordinary law in liberal democracies is unjust, and indeed is bound to be so. By "ordinary" I mean law that (a) does not violate fundamental human rights (e.g., the right not to be tortured or the right against enslavement), and (b) has been enacted via a democratic process that meets certain minimal standards (e.g., no major voting irregularities, no significant suppression of dissent by powerful state or non-state actors, etc.). The focus on ordinary law is thus meant to exclude two kinds of laws: (1) laws that are so seriously and obviously unjust that there can be no sensible or reasonable disagreement about their justness (e.g., laws permitting involuntary slavery), and (2) laws that were not enacted through the approved legislative or judicial process.

How could anyone deny that at least some ordinary laws are unjust? One way to resist this idea is to hold that law, at least in a minimally decent state, *constitutes* justice. On this view, justice is largely indeterminate with regard to specific laws and policies. Justice sets some very general limits on what states can do—for instance, states must refrain from torture, enslavement, or religious persecution—but beyond these minimal constraints, justice does not provide determinate guidance regarding the laws and institutions of a political society. Justice is only rendered determinate by the state's exercise of its legislative, executive, and judicial authority. The law provides a determinate account of citizens' various rights, duties, and legitimate expectations, and this legal regime constitutes justice for that political community. This is a view with roots in Immanuel Kant's political philosophy, and it will be the focus of chapter 3, so I will defer detailed discussion of it until then.

But for now, notice how revisionary the proposal is. If ordinary law—the kind over which people of good faith routinely disagree—cannot be unjust, then much of our existing political discourse involves a conceptual error. This is a radical view of the relationship between disagreement and injustice. The commonsense view is that thoughtful, well-informed people acting in good faith can sometimes be seriously mistaken about justice, and that this explains why ordinary law is sometimes unjust. The view under consideration denies this possibility.

This is another way of stating the obvious: the second claim of our puzzle seems difficult to deny. It's hard to make sense of our political disagreements without this claim. Our political discourse is chock-full of cases where we disagree about whether some law or proposed law is just or unjust. The simplest and most natural explanation of what's happening is that it's sometimes hard to know what justice requires. As a result, our views about justice are sometimes mistaken, even when we are trying in good faith to get it right. Given this kind of disagreement, it's no surprise at all that some of our ordinary laws are unjust.

Legitimate Laws

The term "legitimate" is used by political philosophers in different ways and applied to different subjects.[17] Perhaps most commonly the term is applied to states, rulers, or political regimes that purport to have authority over a given territory. When applied in this way, legitimacy is about the right to rule. There are weaker and stronger versions of this sense of the term. In the weakest sense, to say that some state or regime is legitimate is to say that it typically does not wrong anyone (i.e., it does not infringe anyone's rights) when it issues and coercively enforces rules against those who reside in its territory.

A stronger view holds that a state is legitimate when, in addition to the first condition, those who reside in the territory are presumptively obligated not to interfere with the enforcement of the state's directives and presumptively obligated to obey the state's laws. This is the most familiar notion of legitimacy in the literature, and it has generated one of the largest debates in political philosophy: namely, the debate over whether there can be a presumptive duty to obey the law, at least in reasonable, well-functioning states.

A yet stronger view adds to the two preceding conditions a third: that legitimate states have rights against outsiders (i.e., those not residing in the territory) interfering with their issuing and

17. Influential recent general accounts of political legitimacy include, among others: Applbaum, *Legitimacy*; Buchanan, *Justice, Legitimacy, and Self-Determination*, ch. 5; Simmons, "Justification and Legitimacy"; Stilz, *Liberal Loyalty*.

enforcing of commands within the territory over which the state has jurisdiction.

An even stronger conception of legitimacy adds one further condition: legitimate political authorities have the exclusive right to rule over those within their jurisdiction. No other person or institution has independent permission to issue and enforce rules within the territory and the state is answerable to no higher authority when issuing and enforcing rules that apply within its jurisdiction.

Although there is disagreement about which of the preceding are necessary features of political legitimacy there is no need, for our purposes, to wade into this debate. We can, instead, focus on legitimacy as applied to particular laws or uses of political power. Legitimacy, in this sense, concerns: (1) the moral permission of state officials to apply and enforce a given law or rule, and (2) state officials' moral rights against harmful interference as they perform their authorized roles in applying and enforcing the law. This notion of legitimacy is what's at issue in the puzzle of legitimate injustice. The puzzle is generated by the apparent fact that laws can be legitimate in this sense, and yet also be unjust.[18]

This notion of legitimacy also coheres with a commonsense attitude in liberal democratic societies. Many believe that state officials don't act wrongly, provided that they are applying or enforcing laws or rules that have the appropriate legal or democratic pedigree. Many also believe that state officials are immune from being harmed or attacked for enforcing those laws or policies (provided they are within constitutional limits). State officials are, to invoke a familiar phrase, just doing their jobs, and they don't act wrongly or become liable to harmful interference in virtue of lawfully doing the jobs assigned to them by the democratic process.

---

18. To be clear, the preceding is a stipulative account of what legitimacy is. It is not an account of the moral basis or grounds of legitimacy; it is silent about what justifies or explains why state officials act permissibly in these instances, or why such officials are not liable to harmful interference.

Of course, there are other widely used notions of legitimacy. In particular, legitimacy is sometimes applied to laws in what we can call a "positive procedural" sense. Legitimacy, in this sense, denotes only that a law has been proposed and enacted according to the generally accepted constitutional or legal process. This notion of legitimacy, though useful in various contexts, isn't helpful for thinking about the puzzle of legitimate injustice. It's a purely descriptive claim about positive law—it tells us only that the law was generated via the generally accepted legal process. But this is compatible with holding that such a procedural pedigree is morally inert, or largely irrelevant, to the assignment of moral rights and permissions. Our puzzle arises only if there is, at least an apparent, normative tension between justice and legitimacy. The sense of legitimacy at issue therefore has to be normative—it has to be one that makes claims about the moral status of laws or the officials who apply and enforce them. This doesn't preclude us from considering the moral importance of the procedural pedigree of a law; you might hold that ordinary legislation is legitimate in the moral sense precisely because it is legitimate in the purely procedural sense. But that is a substantive thesis that stands in need of argument (we'll consider various arguments to this effect in later chapters). For the sake of clarity, I think it's helpful to limit our use of the term "legitimacy" to the moral sense I have defined above, and then consider separately what reasons, if any, could explain how ordinary legislation comes to have this moral status.

With that terminological point out of the way, let's return to the third and final claim that constitutes our puzzle, as stated above:

(3) Many [unjust] laws can be legitimate: that is, state officials act permissibly in enforcing these laws and they have rights against harmful interference while enforcing them.

This is probably the most controversial of the three claims. But I suspect it is more controversial amongst professional philosophers than amongst laypersons. Consider an American citizen who has fairly progressive views on matters of economic justice—someone who holds that justice requires much more redistribution of wealth than is currently mandated by American law. Here's a nice illustrative statement of this view from Bernie Sanders's website: "The richest 10 percent of households have 70 percent of the wealth. The top 1% have increased their share of the wealth from 23% in 1989 to nearly 32% in 2018. The three wealthiest people in the U.S. own more wealth than the bottom 50% of Americans—160 million people. Bernie believes this is unjust and is calling for a downward transfer of wealth."[19] Bernie Sanders, and presumably many of those who voted for him in his bids to become the Democratic nominee for president, believe the current distribution of income and wealth in the United States is unjust. But neither Sanders, nor those who supported him, were necessarily claiming that existing US laws structuring the tax code and provision of economic benefits were morally illegitimate. They were not arguing that state officials applying these laws were acting impermissibly, nor were they suggesting that such officials were liable to be harmed.

This is one example, but there are countless others where many ordinary citizens apparently endorse some version of the third claim in our puzzle: for example, in debates over socialized medicine, immigration law, or climate policy. In each case there are people who sincerely hold the view that the existing law is unjust—indeed sometimes extremely unjust—and yet also appear sincerely to accept the view that state officials can permissibly enforce such laws and have rights against harmful interference. Those most likely to resist the third claim are people in the grip of a philosophical theory, one that yokes legitimacy and justice very tightly together. But most non-philosophers aren't in the grip of a philosophical theory about the relationship between justice and legitimacy, and so are more likely to be comfortable accepting the possibility of legitimate injustice.

Of course, the mere fact that many people accept a claim doesn't mean that it's true, or even philosophically defensible. But there are plenty of respectable-looking arguments in support of this third claim. Some hold the third claim to be true because political institutions—at least of a certain type—have crucial instrumental value in realizing good outcomes such as peace, stability, and protection of the rule of law. Alternatively, some defend the third claim on the basis that democratic institutions are essential to fairly resolve political disputes, or that such institutions are essential to instantiate egalitarian or nonhierarchical social relations. We will examine these arguments more closely in chapters 4 and 5, including reasons to be skeptical about them.

But at this stage I only wish to emphasize that many laypersons and philosophers are inclined to accept the third claim. Moreover, as I will argue in chapter 2, the theoretical and practical costs of rejecting the third claim are steep. I am skeptical that a diverse political society can function in a fair or effective manner if we reject the third claim—if citizens endorse the view that state officials act wrongly whenever they apply and enforce unjust laws, and that such officials are therefore liable to harmful interference.

Dismissing the Puzzle

The subsequent chapters of the book examine how different influential accounts of political morality might explain the puzzle of legitimate injustice or dissolve it by rejecting one of its core claims. But before we get to that, I want to consider two initial attempts to dismiss the puzzle altogether—attempts to show, in effect, there's nothing puzzling here in the slightest; that all three claims can easily or obviously be affirmed.

Recall the three claims that constitute the puzzle:

1) "Justice is the first virtue of social institutions, as truth is of systems of thought. A theory however elegant and economical must be rejected or revised if it is untrue; likewise laws and institutions no matter how efficient and

well-arranged must be reformed or abolished if they are unjust."[20]

2) Some ordinary laws in liberal democratic societies are unjust.

3) Many of these laws can be legitimate: that is, state officials act permissibly in enforcing these laws and they have rights against harmful interference while enforcing them.

You might object that there's no formal inconsistency between the claims, and so no real puzzle. Rawls says unjust laws must be reformed or abolished, but this doesn't logically entail that it is impermissible for state officials to impose unjust laws. A skeptic might claim the puzzle can be dissolved if we hold that the obligation to reform or abolish unjust laws does not fall on the state officials who enforce the laws, but rather only on officials in the legislatures (and other entities) that enact them, or the courts that interpret or review them. But while this division of labor might show that there's no logical contradiction between the three claims, it doesn't explain the phenomenon of legitimate injustice. If justice is the first virtue of social institutions, why should state officials, but not legislatures and courts, be allowed to disregard its requirements when imposing laws on citizens? Shouldn't everyone, especially those wielding significant political power, abide by the requirements of justice? How can we sensibly say that a law must be reformed or abolished while also insisting it can be permissibly imposed by those in power? Maybe there are answers to these questions, but figuring them out means solving the puzzle. So the puzzle doesn't disappear just by pointing out the lack of formal inconsistency.

Maybe we should instead dismiss the puzzle because the three claims operate or apply at different levels of ideal or non-ideal theory. More specifically, you might think the first claim about justice applies only under conditions of full compliance: that is,

20. Rawls, *Theory of Justice*, 3.

conditions whereby everyone, or nearly everyone, acts in accordance with the requirements of justice. Under conditions of full compliance perhaps it's true that justice is the first virtue of social institutions, but this claim isn't true once we stipulate significant levels of non-compliance or wrongdoing. But the second and third claims seem to presuppose significant non-compliance. Once we stipulate that there are unjust laws, we're in the realm of non-ideal theory. So there's no puzzle, since the normative injunctions in ideal theory must differ from the normative injunctions under non-ideal conditions.

Although I think this suggestion points us in the right direction, it doesn't dissolve the puzzle—it doesn't explain how the three claims can all be comfortably affirmed. Why would some degree of non-compliance suddenly change the relationship between justice and other considerations, depriving justice of its lexical priority? Indeed, when faced with at least some problems of non-compliance, most of us are not tempted to abandon the priority of justice. We know that some people cheat on their taxes, but it doesn't follow that we should no longer accord justice priority when designing the tax code. We know that some people commit heinous crimes such as murder and rape, but it doesn't follow that our criminal justice system should prioritize other values at the expense of respecting individual rights. Perhaps there is a story that can explain why, under some levels of non-compliance, justice should no longer be the first virtue of our social institutions. But this is no easy way to dismiss the puzzle. Such a story amounts to a substantive and controversial thesis about how the three claims can be reconciled; one that stands in need of justification.

Aims and Scope

Before providing an overview of the chapters to follow, I want to say something about the scope of the book, and how it relates to the broader landscape of political philosophy.

This book is emphatically not a comprehensive introduction to contemporary political philosophy. There's no attempt to cover the vast range of topics that have received sustained attention in the recent literature. Indeed, the sub-field is now far too broad and diverse for this to be a realistic ambition for any single text. Although this book focuses on the puzzle of legitimate injustice, it does not engage in great detail with the large literature on more specific questions about principles of distributive justice. One question concerns the content of such principles. Does distributive justice require equality, sufficiency, priority for the worst off, or something else entirely? A second question concerns the currency of distribution: what is getting distributed by principles of justice? Is it external resources, welfare, freedom from the power of others, capabilities to perform key functions, or some combination of all of these? Relatedly, there's a lively debate about the extent to which principles of justice must be responsibility-sensitive. There is also a question about the scope of distributive principles. Do they, for instance, apply across political borders, or only within each political community? Do the principles apply intergenerationally?

Some also reject the very idea that justice is fundamentally, or primarily, distributive. Relational or social egalitarians hold that justice requires establishing egalitarian, or non-hierarchical, social relations. The distribution of goods or advantages will sometimes be relevant to securing such relations, but the distribution is not the point—it only matters insofar as it helps to establish the relevant relations of equality.[21]

This book, will not, for the most part, be wading into these debates. I assume that justice requires an appropriate (I will often use "fair") distribution of the relevant currency, but this assumption is consistent with relational accounts of justice, since it

---

21. For an illuminating recent attempt to reconceptualize the debate between so-called distributive and relational theories of justice, see Schouten, *Anatomy of Justice*, esp. chs. 1–4.

remains neutral about the more fundamental explanation of why appropriate distributions are required by justice. I also assume, at various points, that particular goods or advantages are part of the currency of social or distributive justice, but these assumptions will be, for the most part, uncontroversial. Few deny, for example, that the distribution of income, wealth, or civil and political liberties are matters of justice.

The book also has nothing to say about the geographic scope of justice. I will talk about justice and legitimacy within a political society or community, but this is for ease of exposition—the puzzle of legitimate injustice is going to arise regardless of whether the scope of justice is global or more local.

There are also many more specific or applied questions about justice that don't receive much, if any, attention in the chapters to follow. These topics include (to name only a few): the justification of criminal punishment; racial justice; just war theory; animal rights; environmental justice; immigration; and the use of algorithms and artificial intelligence. But although the book doesn't engage with particular applied issues, the more abstract question of how to conceptualize the relationship between justice and legitimacy has significant implications for these topics.

I also want to emphasize a few things about the approach and method of the book to avoid disappointing readers who may have been expecting something else. This book does not offer a survey or overview of leading ideologies or "isms" in politics. If you're looking for a text that analyzes and compares influential theories of liberalism, socialism, libertarianism, and so on . . . this is not the book for you.

There is also no discussion of act utilitarian theories of political morality, or simple act consequentialist theories more generally. There are at least two reasons for this. First, the puzzle of legitimate injustice doesn't arise for such views. If each agent is directed to maximize utility, then the only puzzle there can ever be is working out which option, from the available alternatives, in fact brings about the most good. There's no interesting question about how

injustice could be legitimate. Second, simple forms of act consequentialism have not been very influential in political philosophy.
One reason for this, I suspect, is that the institutions and rules of
political life are not plausibly explicable by reference to such theories. Their moral import has to be understood in some other way.
There are also various methodological or meta-philosophical
debates that are not a focus of this book. One issue that has occupied a great deal of attention in recent years is the distinction
between ideal and non-ideal theory. A lot of ink has been spilled
over how to draw this distinction, and yet more has been spilled
over which kind of political philosophy (ideal or non-ideal)
should be the focus of our discipline. I have views about these issues, but rather than argue for them here, I'm just going to lay my
cards on the table. My view is that there is no single, canonical, "correct" way to draw the distinction between ideal and non-ideal
theory. There is instead a plurality of dimensions along which our
theories of political morality can vary with regard to how realistic
or non-realistic its assumptions can be. Theories can be more,
or less, realistic with regard to the degree to which parties comply,
the degree to which agents behave altruistically, the level of resources available, the degree of information available, and techno-
logical limitations, as well as various other dimensions.[22] Because
there are so many different ways in which theories can be more, or
less, ideal, I'm skeptical that there's a uniquely correct answer to
the question of whether political philosophers ought to be con-
centrating primarily on ideal or on non-ideal theory. There are
good reasons to engage in different kinds of political philosophy,
some of which will be heavily idealized along multiple dimensions, and some of which will be much more realistic along many
dimensions: it all depends on the more specific aims of the
theorist.

22. For helpful discussions of the distinction between ideal and non-ideal theory,
see, for example, Hamlin and Stemplowska, "Theory, Ideal Theory"; Valentini, "Ideal
vs. Non-ideal Theory."

Another meta-philosophical debate that has received a fair bit of attention, but about which this book has little to say, is that between so-called realism and moralism within political philosophy.[23] It's notoriously difficult to pin down exactly what this debate is supposed to be about, but I think that if it is about anything substantive, it is the following idea. Realists maintain that the domain of political morality is in some sense *sui generis*: the rules or principles that apply in politics are not derivable from, or reducible to, morality outside the political realm. Realists sometimes insist that there is something about the nature of political life, or its practices, that serves as the unique source of political normativity, a source that isn't reducible to more general moral values or principles. Differing realists then offer more specific claims about the distinctive nature of political morality. Moralists, by contrast, view political philosophy as a particular branch of moral philosophy—as simply one of several domains where general moral principles or truths must be worked out.

Again, because I lack the space to properly engage with these claims, I'll state my view without defending it. I think that there are normative questions and puzzles—for example, about the collective use of power to set rules for everyone—that are distinctive to politics. I thus agree there are questions for political philosophy that have no precise analog in non-political moral theory, and so the answers will be, in some sense, distinctive to political philosophy. But I don't believe political philosophy is *sui generis* in the way that at least some realists seem to hold. The solutions to political philosophy's distinctive puzzles depend on moral values or ideals that are not distinctive to the political realm. Freedom, equality, and fairness, for example, are central political values, but they aren't distinctive to, or limited to, the political realm. Since I

23. For an overview of realism, see Rossi and Sleat, "Realism in Normative Political Theory." For a discussion of the contrast between realism and moralism, and a defense of an alternative middle ground, see Larmore, *What Is Political Philosophy?*.

don't think we can solve the central normative questions in political philosophy without appeal to such values, I don't agree with the realist thesis, at least the version of it described above. Having made some deflationary remarks about the book's scope and aims, let me say something more positive about what it does aim to do.

Theories of justice purport to tell us about the rightful allocation of freedom and other advantages amongst persons. There's a widely shared assumption that justice has a special priority in political life—we can't choose unjust institutions to better realize some other goals. Theories of political legitimacy purport to tell us under what conditions some people or institutions can rightfully wield enormous power over others; issuing and enforcing commands over a very wide range of our social life. To put it differently, theories of justice and legitimacy each claim to tell us how political rules and institutions can be rightfully organized. But justice and legitimacy are typically presented as having different normative bases. Theories of legitimacy are often procedural or historical in nature. That is, legitimacy is typically held to reside either in the procedural pedigree of a law or command, or in some historical fact about the relationship between those who issue the command and those to whom the command is supposed to apply. At least some principles of justice, on the other hand, are widely assumed to be true independent of such procedural or historical facts. The result is that justice and legitimacy seem likely to conflict. Indeed, given certain plausible assumptions, they're going to conflict on a regular basis. We thus won't have a clear picture of political morality without understanding the relationship between justice and legitimacy and how their apparently conflicting claims are to be adjudicated. Focusing on the puzzle of legitimate injustice is thus one way to tackle what I take to be one of the central issues, indeed perhaps the central issue, in political philosophy.

The chapters that follow examine different ways of addressing the puzzle. We learn new and important things, I believe, by looking at some of the recent literature through the lens of legitimate injustice. Too often theories of justice or theories of legitimacy are assessed in isolation from each other. By asking what different views tell us about legitimate injustice, we get a clearer and deeper picture of the strengths and weakness of different theories. Does a theory require us to give up one of the three claims listed above, or does it promise some reconciliation of them, and if so, how is that reconciliation to be achieved? I hope that addressing these questions illuminates some of the landscape of political philosophy in ways that are novel and fruitful.

Overview

Here is a quick overview of the rest of the book.

One way to resolve the puzzle of legitimate injustice is to deny the third claim. On this view, individual moral rights are sacrosanct. When governments enact and enforce unjust laws, they act impermissibly and the relevant officials lack rights against harmful interference with the enforcement of such laws. Chapter 2 considers this view.

Although this position has the virtues of clarity and simplicity, I argue that we ought to reject it. It entails that public officials, acting in good faith and enforcing laws with an accepted procedural pedigree, are regularly guilty of serious wrongdoing. It also entails, given certain other plausible premises, that citizens might permissibly use necessary and proportionate harmful force against public officials who attempt to enforce democratically enacted but substantively unjust tax policies, safety regulations, or environmental regulations. These implications are very counterintuitive, and they point us to the deeper problem with this view: it has nothing to say about how groups of sincere and thoughtful people are supposed to live peaceably together when they disagree about what justice requires.

Some contemporary Kantians dissolve the puzzle by rejecting the second claim: that many ordinary laws in liberal democratic societies are unjust. On this view, the focus of chapter 3, the requirements of justice are largely indeterminate in the absence of laws issued by an impartial public authority. Conclusive individual rights are only established when a state serves as the impartial adjudicator to resolve problems of moral indeterminacy and lack of assurance. The laws of a suitably legitimate state thus cannot be unjust. Instead, the law in such a state renders the requirements of justice determinate. To be sure, some goals or policies are so gravely at odds with securing the mutual independence of persons that no legitimate state can permissibly pursue them. But once those cases are set aside, there can be no gap between legitimate law and justice—the one constitutes the other.

Although it has much to recommend it, I argue that we should not accept this picture. Most importantly, I argue that the Kantian view is vulnerable to a dilemma. To vindicate the idea that political institutions are uniquely constitutive of just relations between persons, the Kantian must make some very sweeping and implausible claims about the extent to which justice is indeterminate. On the other hand, if the Kantian makes more modest assumptions about the extent to which justice is indeterminate, it's no longer clear that other essential aspects of the Kantian view—in particular the claim that the unilateral use of force is never fully rightful—can be sustained.

Chapter 4 examines theories that focus on the instrumental value of political institutions, in particular the instrumental value of relations of authority. Consider Joseph Raz's hugely influential normal justification thesis:[24]

the normal way to establish that a person has authority over another person involves showing that the alleged subject is likely better to comply with reasons which apply to him [. . .] if he accepts the directives of the alleged authority as authoritatively binding and tries to follow them, rather than by trying to follow the reasons which apply to him directly.

Here's how this might help to explain legitimate injustice. If state officials generally comply better with the reasons that apply to them by accepting the directives issued by their superiors as authoritative, rather than by engaging in first-order deliberation, then the superiors have legitimate practical authority over those officials. This is true even if there will be some cases where the directives are mistaken. If some of the mistaken directives are mistakes about justice, this could explain how government officials can legitimately enforce unjust laws.

This proposal, however, is confronted by a version of the rule worship objection that plagues rule consequentialism. It's true that if I can better comply with the reasons that apply to me by following the directives of the authority than by trying to decide things for myself, following the directives of the authority is the right thing to do. But when the authority is in fact mistaken, it's odd to assert that I still have a justification for complying with the mistaken directive simply because, as a general matter, following the authority's directives is a good rule. We do have reasons for adopting the rule, but these reasons are merely instrumental, and only imperfectly track the more fundamental considerations. When the two come apart in particular instances, there's no justification for following a purely instrumental rule that fails to deliver its promised benefits. I call this the *bridging problem*.

Chapter 5 turns to consider a family of views that make claims about the intrinsic or non-instrumental value of democracy. These theories identify some egalitarian property of democratic institutions that is held to be non-instrumentally valuable and claim that value grounds the authority of democratic decisions, an authority that might explain the phenomenon of legitimate injustice. Some of these views reject the first claim of the puzzle—that justice is the first virtue of social institutions. But other versions promise a resolution of the puzzle without abandoning any of its claims.

All such views, however, face the same problem. Whatever property is identified as having non-instrumental value—the public manifestation of equality, equal respect, or relations of social equality—it's a further question whether this value is sufficiently weighty to justify committing injustice in the range of cases where democratic institutions are typically deemed to possess authority. It is difficult to see why the non-instrumental value of democratic decisions is likely—over a defined range of issues—to have greater weight than the disvalue of injustice. I call this the *weighing problem.*

The weighing problem is particularly acute once we recognize that the very same feature of democratic institutions that is held to be non-instrumentally valuable can also be undermined by the democratic enactment of unjust laws. Egalitarian relationships can be threatened not only by a failure to respect egalitarian decision procedures, but also by inegalitarian distributions of income and wealth, or inegalitarian access to important medical services. Similarly, we may fail to show equal respect to persons when we fail to respect democratic decisions, but we surely also fail to show equal respect to some persons when we unjustly imprison them for using recreational drugs, or when we unjustly deny some people a fair opportunity to educate themselves.

Finally, in chapter 6, I look at how we might explain legitimate injustice by appeal to distributive justice itself. After considering and rejecting a recent proposal by Daniel Viehoff grounded in distributive fairness, I offer my own view. Suppose that disagreement about politics is intractable even amongst intelligent, well-meaning, and well-informed persons. If this is true, we can anticipate that even in highly idealized circumstances, unjust legislation is practically unavoidable. Citizens won't agree on many important political questions, and there is no effective way to ensure that political power will be exercised only in accordance with the true requirements of justice.

If unjust legislation in a cooperative society is unavoidable, even under very favorable conditions, then it constitutes a burden of cooperative life that, like other such burdens, must be distributed in accordance with just principles. My suggestion is that justice requires that we collectively share in the responsibility for this burden, and doing so requires making room for legitimate injustice. In designing our political institutions we know that unjust laws will be passed, and thus constitute a burden on members of the political community. But the special challenge we face is this: we will never agree about which specific laws constitute the unjust burdens. To handle this unusual kind of distributive problem, we must allow the results of the democratic process to take priority when resolving disagreements that fall within certain parameters. As Rawls says, "we submit our conduct to democratic authority only to the extent necessary to share equitably in the inevitable imperfections of a constitutional system. Accepting these hardships is simply recognizing and being willing to work within the limits imposed by the circumstances of human life."[25] Legitimate injustice is thus something mandated by justice itself—it's required as a solution to the inevitable fact that we cannot design political institutions that do not err.

On this view, the puzzle of legitimate injustice is resolved by showing that justice and legitimacy are not, or at least not completely, two competing values that need to be balanced or traded off against each other. Instead, the content and limits of political legitimacy arise partly out of a commitment to the just allocation of the benefits and burdens of cooperative life.

25. Rawls, *Theory of Justice*, 312.

2

Let Justice Be Done

OUR WORLD IS replete with examples of serious injustice: the persecution of religious minorities; systemic racism; the denial of equal political and civil rights to women and LGBTQ persons; or the criminalization of conduct that should not be criminalized, such as the possession of certain recreational drugs. Agents of the state who perpetrate these injustices act wrongly and ordinary citizens are not under a moral duty to refrain from interfering. No one, merely by virtue of being a government official, has a moral pass to commit injustice. Let's call this view *Justice First*.

Justice First is simple, intuitive, and rooted in powerful ideas about morality and politics. It also dissolves the puzzle of legitimate injustice. That puzzle, recall, is generated by the following three claims:

1) "Justice is the first virtue of social institutions, as truth is of systems of thought. A theory however elegant and economical must be rejected or revised if it is untrue; likewise laws and institutions no matter how efficient and well-arranged must be reformed or abolished if they are unjust."[1]

2) Some ordinary laws in liberal democratic societies are unjust.

1. Rawls, *Theory of Justice*, 3.

33

3) Many of these laws can be legitimate: that is, state officials act permissibly in enforcing these laws and they have rights against harmful interference while enforcing them.

Although each claim is plausible and accepted by many, they are collectively in tension. But there is no puzzle, according to Justice First, since the third claim is false: state officials typically do not act permissibly in enforcing unjust laws, and they typically do not have claim rights against harmful interference with their enforcement.

Justice First is also a view with a distinguished pedigree. Thomas Aquinas, John Locke, Immanuel Kant, Martin Luther King Jr., John Rawls, and Robert Nozick, to name only a few prominent examples, all make claims that might be interpreted as expressing support for Justice First. More recently, Jason Brennan, Ryan Davis, Gerhard Øverland and Christian Barry, Bas van der Vossen, and Kit Wellman have all offered arguments that provide some support for Justice First.[2] In doing so, they sometimes draw upon Jeff McMahan's influential views regarding the ethics of harming and killing in war.[3]

This chapter examines Justice First. To begin, I render the view more precise, explain its appeal, and present the main arguments in its favor. But the chapter also subjects the view to critical scrutiny. I argue that there are very serious costs to accepting Justice First. Most obviously, it conflicts sharply with a commonsense view of what government officials are doing when they faithfully perform their democratically authorized roles. Furthermore,

---

2. Brennan, *When All Else Fails*; Davis, "Justice: Do It"; Øverland and Barry, "Do Democratic Societies Have a Right"; van der Vossen, "Consent"; Wellman, "Space Between." Candice Delmas and Avia Pasternak have also each recently advanced arguments in favor of the permissibility of violently resisting some unjust laws; however, I do not include them as proponents of Justice First, since their arguments are more narrowly focused on the permissibility of violent resistance, and also more narrowly tailored to certain circumstances. See Delmas, *Duty to Resist*; Pasternak, *No Justice*.

3. McMahan, *Killing in War*.

Justice First has radically revisionary implications concerning officials' liability to be harmed. It entails, for example, that ordinary citizens will often be permitted to attack or even kill government officials who are acting in good faith, and merely executing democratically enacted legislation. Finally, Justice First struggles to address the fact of pervasive political disagreement. This undermines the practical relevance of the view, but it also threatens to render it incoherent. My conclusion is that while Justice First presents a powerful challenge to several prominent theories of political morality, the view creates at least as many serious problems as it solves.

Justice First

The famous Latin phrase from which this chapter draws its title is "Fiat iūstitia ruat cælum," which translates as "Let justice be done though the heavens fall." It gives expression to the idea that justice takes precedence no matter how bad the consequences may be. Immanuel Kant approvingly mentions a variant of this principle,[4] and Kant's moral and political philosophy is sometimes presented as congruent with this idea. For example, Kant holds that it is impermissible to violate perfect duties of justice, such as promissory duties, even when doing so will have disastrous consequences. John Rawls also seems to express this idea, in saying that "[e]ach person possesses an inviolability founded on justice that even the welfare of society as a whole cannot override."[5] Robert Nozick's idea of rights as side-constraints might be interpreted as a version of Justice First. As he says, the "side-constraint view forbids you to violate these moral constraints in the pursuit of your goals."[6] And Martin Luther King Jr., in various speeches and interviews, argued that there is no duty to obey an unjust law;

4. Kant, "Perpetual Peace, 123.
5. Rawls, *Theory of Justice*, 3.
6. Nozick, *Anarchy, State, and Utopia*, 29.

rather there is a moral duty to disobey unjust laws.[7] In doing so, he drew upon Christian theologians such as Augustine and Aquinas.

All these thinkers are expressing some version of the idea that justice must take precedence over other considerations. But we need to untangle different possible formulations of this idea to clarify what the best formulation of the Justice First view might be. Let's begin with the most sweeping version:

Maximal Priority: Justice has lexical priority over all considerations for all agents in all contexts.

This principle is maximal in two ways. First, it accords justice lexical priority over all other considerations. Second, this lexically prime status is unrestricted in scope—it applies to all agents in all contexts.

This principle, however, is extremely implausible: it's very difficult to believe that justice is maximal in either of these two ways. Even those of us who accord great weight to individual rights typically concede that there are some circumstances where individual rights can be permissibly infringed. These are circumstances where disastrous, or at least sufficiently terrible, consequences will occur if we do not infringe some people's moral rights. So-called *lesser-evil justifications* endorse infringing moral rights in such circumstances. Many believe, for example, that it can be permissible to redirect a lethal threat (e.g., a runaway trolley, a rockslide, a bomb), away from a large number of people and toward a much smaller number of people, even though doing this will infringe the rights of the smaller number. The idea is that moral rights provide a robust, but defeasible, constraint against being harmed or interfered with for the sake of some greater good. It is not permissible to infringe a person's rights to bring about some modestly better outcome, but if the consequences are sufficiently grave, then it does become permissible to infringe at least some claims of justice.

7. See, for example, King, *Letter from Birmingham Jail*.

LET JUSTICE BE DONE 37

Maximal Priority denies this, and is thus committed to wildly counterintuitive conclusions; for example, that it's not permissible to save twenty thousand (or two hundred thousand, or twenty million) lives by redirecting flood waters away from the twenty thousand (or two hundred thousand, or twenty million) toward a single innocent person in the valley below.

Maximal Priority also delivers counterintuitive results regarding the scope of justice. Suppose that your neighbor is a curmudgeon who is very insistent about his property rights. He does not give permission to others to enter his back garden, and he's told you in no uncertain terms you are never allowed to enter his garden, even to retrieve one of your child's toys. But one afternoon (when your neighbor is away for several days), your child throws her favorite toy over the garden face and becomes inconsolable that she can't get the toy back. May you briefly enter the neighbor's garden to retrieve the toy even though you know the neighbor would not grant permission? Doing so is an infringement of his property rights, but some will say that there is something about the role of parenthood and/ or the context of being neighbors that renders this minor injustice morally permissible in the circumstances.

The proponent of Maximal Priority can try and evade these sorts of troubling counterexamples. They can insist that we never have rights against others' acts when their acts are morally permissible. Thus, even if it would normally be a violation of a person's rights to redirect a flood toward them and kill them, in the circumstance where this is the only way to save twenty thousand lives, the person in question does not have a right against being killed in this way. On this view, the rights we have are very context-sensitive. This is sometimes referred to as *specificationism* about rights.[8]

But Maximal Priority combined with specificationism offers only a hollow victory to those who argue that state officials cannot permissibly impose unjust laws and policies. The victory is hollow

---

8. See, for example, Liberto, "Moral Specification of Rights"; Oberdiek, "Specifying Rights."

since the view will declare it permissible for state officials to do all kinds of things that are intuitively unjust, while insisting that whatever state officials permissibly do cannot in fact be unjust. Such a view is Justice First in name only. In sum, the proponent of Maximal Priority is either committed to some deeply implausible claims about what is permissible, or else they avoid this only at the cost of hollowing out the content of Justice First by adopting specificationism about rights.

But few defend Maximal Priority, and proponents of Justice First don't need to embrace such a sweeping thesis. They only need to insist that the claims of justice typically take precedence over other claims, and more specifically, that government officials do not gain permission to commit injustice merely by virtue of their official role, and others are not duty-bound to refrain from using otherwise permissible forms of defensive harm to prevent such officials from acting unjustly. It's helpful to separate Justice First into two distinct arguments:

Impermissibility Argument

1) State officials are on a par with ordinary citizens with regard to the moral permission to commit injustice.
2) Ordinary citizens are not morally permitted to commit injustice for any of the reasons typically advanced to justify acts of legitimate injustice by state officials.

Therefore,

3) The acts standardly understood as instances of legitimate injustice are not, in fact, morally permissible.

Liability Argument

4) State officials are on a par with ordinary citizens with regard to liability to harmful interference when they commit injustice.
5) Ordinary citizens are, in principle, liable to harmful interference if they perform unjust acts for any of the

reasons typically advanced to justify acts of legitimate injustice by state officials.

Therefore,

6) State officials are, in principle, liable to harmful interference when they commit the acts standardly understood as instances of legitimate injustice.

Versions of these arguments have recently been advanced by Jason Brennan, Jeff McMahan, Gerhard Øverland and Christian Barry, and Kit Wellman, among others.[9] Together these arguments constitute what I'm calling Justice First. They purport to establish that there's no such thing as legitimate injustice in the sense that is our focus. Government officials are, on this view, no different than ordinary citizens when it comes to committing injustice. Ordinary citizens are typically not permitted to wrongfully harm or imprison innocent people and are liable to harmful interference if they try to do so. The same is true of government officials. Unlike Maximal Priority, these arguments do not require the implausible assumption that justice takes precedence in every context. Proponents of these arguments can concede that justice must sometimes give way to other considerations. They simply deny that government officials, qua officials, somehow gain permission to commit injustice, and have claims against harmful interference, that ordinary citizens lack. There is, in this respect, nothing special about being a state official.

The Case for Justice First

Consider the following story:

Weed: Albert owns his own home in a residential neighborhood. One of the nice features of Albert's house is a large back yard. One day Albert discovers an unusual weed growing in his yard which, when smoked, is moderately intoxicating.

9. See notes 2 and 3 above.

Smoking the weed in his home becomes something Albert enjoys doing to relax (he poses no risk to others in doing so). Some of the other residents in Albert's neighborhood, however, are puritanical and they decide they do not want Albert smoking this weed in their neighborhood. They inform Albert that they have got together to discuss things, and a majority voted that smoking this weed won't be tolerated in the neighborhood any longer. Albert doesn't agree with this decision, but the majority of his neighbors say his refusal is irrelevant—they will just break into his home and take his weed if he doesn't comply.

Let's stipulate that what the neighbors threaten to do is unjust. Albert, after all, is using weeds that grow on his own property and he isn't posing any risk of harm to anyone else. The neighbors are threatening to infringe Albert's rights simply because they don't like something that he does in the privacy of his own home. The neighbors' threat is not only unjust, it's impermissible: there's no sufficient justification for infringing Albert's rights in this way. Since the neighbors threaten to act unjustly and impermissibly, it also seems true that Albert is under no obligation to let them behave in this way; he could use necessary and proportionate force to defend himself from their wrongful threat.

Here's another example:

Family Separation: Bianca intends to move so that she can live in the same town as her grandmother and help care for her as she gets older. But when Bianca gets within a few miles of the town a group of local townspeople stop her car and tell her she's not allowed to proceed any further. They have decided their town is "full already" and anyway they don't want more people from Bianca's culture moving in and changing the character of their town. Bianca tries to insist, but a couple of the townspeople pull out weapons and tell her to turn around and leave or they will indefinitely "detain" her in a makeshift and unsafe-looking "camp" they have set up by the side of the road.

Here again, we can stipulate that what the townspeople are doing is unjust and impermissible. They cannot permissibly threaten Bianca with force to interfere with her freedom of movement and choice of where to live. And since they are wrongfully threatening her it would seem that Bianca is, in principle, permitted to use necessary and proportionate force to defend herself. Proponents of Justice First take cases like Weed and Family Separation—cases where private individuals threaten to act in ways that are unjust and impermissible—and argue that there's no relevant difference between these cases and apparently analogous cases where government officials threaten to act in the same way. The proponent of Justice First thus effectively puts the burden of proof on their opponent. The opponent is challenged to find some morally relevant difference between otherwise analogous injustices committed by private persons and government officials, but proponents of Justice First argue that this challenge cannot be met.[10]

There are many ways to try and establish a difference between what the private individuals do in Weed and Family Separation, and what similarly situated government officials might do. I won't survey all these arguments now, in part because some of them will receive more detailed treatment in chapters 3–6. Rather, we only need to look at some examples to gain a better appreciation for the structure and appeal of the Justice First position.

Consent

To begin, one might appeal to consent. Neither Albert nor Bianca agreed to be bound by the authority of the neighbors or the townspeople. Since they did not consent, there is no moral basis for the neighbors or townspeople to control Albert's and Bianca's

10. Brennan most explicitly pursues this strategy in *When All Else Fails*, though Øverland and Barry, and Wellman, pursue broadly similar strategies. See Øverland and Barry, "Do Democratic Societies Have a Right"; Wellman, "Space Between."

decisions. But governments—at least some governments—are different. We agree to be bound by the laws and regulations of the country in which we reside. Government officials in those countries, at least those acting within the parameters of their roles, thus gain moral liberties to impose rules, even unjust rules, and to enjoy immunities from harmful interference, that the neighbors and townspeople lack.

There are, however, many well-known and serious problems with this proposal.[11] The first problem is simple: most people do not consent to the authority of their government. Children cannot consent to the authority of their government, and when we reach the stage where consent is finally possible, most people do not consent to their government's authority; they simply continue to reside in the country in which they were born.

In light of the absence of widespread express consent, some shift the focus to tacit consent. Perhaps we tacitly consent to the government's authority when we do (or fail to do) certain things: for example, when we decide to remain a resident in the country in which we are born. But the fact that someone refuses to leave is hardly sufficient to show that they have consented to the existing de facto ruler's authority. As Hume famously points out, you have not consented to the captain's authority if you suddenly find yourself on a ship in the middle of the ocean and you refuse to walk the plank.[12] For a decision to constitute morally meaningful tacit consent, various conditions need to be satisfied. One such condition is that the consenter must have a reasonable opportunity to avoid tacitly consenting. For many, perhaps most people, leaving the country in which they were born and raised is a very costly and risky option. Moreover, this appeal to tacit consent does not distinguish what a government official might do from what the neighbors threaten to do to Albert in Weed. The neighbors might claim

11. Brennan highlights many of these problems in *When All Else Fails*, 72–76.
12. Hume, "Of the Original Contract."

Albert has tacitly consented to their rules by choosing to remain a resident in the neighborhood.

Finally, even if we set the preceding problems aside, consent does not explain how government officials are permitted to act unjustly. Suppose A enlists in the army, and consents to follow the orders of his commanding officer, B. Prior to receiving A's consent, B could not permissibly enforce rules on A—if he did so he would be violating A's moral rights. After A consents, things are different. A no longer has moral rights against B enforcing various commands (at least within a certain scope). Now when B enforces directives on A (e.g., to clean the latrines, or run for six miles) B isn't infringing any moral rights of A's; A waived those moral rights when he enlisted in the army. Consent thus has the power to transform acts that would have been rights infringements into noninfringements. B doesn't commit injustices against A when his commands stay within the scope of A's consent.

In sum, appeal to the consent of the governed is not a promising way to explain how state officials could permissibly commit injustice, nor how they might be immune from harmful interference.[13] Most people don't consent to the authority of state institutions, but even if they did, this would establish that state officials, acting ex officio, don't commit injustice at all when enforcing the laws and policies of the government within the scope of that consent.

Doing One's Job

Government officials, even when enforcing unjust laws and policies, are "just doing their job." They are aren't acting as vigilantes; they are rather acting in an official capacity and (in constitutional democracies, at least) they are acting on behalf of the public.

---

13. For an argument in support of the conclusion that consent cannot ground a duty to obey unjust institutions, see van der Vossen, "Consent."

Perhaps this explains why state officials are not morally on a par with ordinary citizens in committing injustice? To assess the plausibility of this claim, we need to be more precise. What is it, exactly, about "doing one's job" that is supposed to be morally relevant? One possibility is that state officials are mere instruments—they are simply carrying out orders that have been authorized by others. Because they are mere instruments in this way, perhaps they do not act impermissibly and/or are not liable to harm when they carry out injustice others have authorized?

But this, as many have argued, is not a credible position.[14] If your boss tells you to violate someone else's rights, you cannot evade the charge of wrongdoing by saying that you are simply your boss's instrument. You are a moral agent, not an inanimate object being wielded by your boss. Mafia hit men, for example, do not evade the charge of wrongdoing by virtue of the fact that they are merely following orders. Sometimes the fact that you are merely following orders can mitigate the extent to which you are to blame for wrongful acts. This is true, for example, if you are likely to face negative consequences for disobedience. If the hit man is himself going to be killed if he doesn't comply, he is not nearly as blameworthy as he would be if he faced no duress. But to say that someone isn't as blameworthy doesn't entail that they haven't acted wrongly. On the contrary, it presupposes that they have acted wrongly.

To make the appeal to "doing one's job" more compelling, we must restrict its scope. Perhaps doing one's job *as a government official within a constitutional democracy* is what creates special permissions and immunities with regard to injustice. But although this restriction on scope helps to avoid some counterexamples, the puzzle remains. If doing one's job does not, as a general principle, create these permissions and immunities, how could it do so when one acts as the agent of a constitutional, democratic community? If it can do so, that must be because of features of democracy or

---

14. Jeff McMahan is the most influential current critic of this suggestion. See, for example, McMahan, *Killing in War*, 84–91.

constitutional democracy, rather than the mere fact that state officials are doing their jobs. To assess the proposal we will therefore have to consider the significance of democracy more directly.

Democracy

In cases of extreme and obvious injustice, the fact that a democratic majority has authorized the injustice does nothing to render its enforcement permissible. If democratic majorities voted to enact slavery, or racial segregation, or the persecution of religious minorities, this would not render the enforcement of such policies morally permissible, nor give the enforcing officials immunity from harmful interference. Even the most strident proponents of the value of democracy are likely to concede this much.

But if this is true, then why should any form of injustice at all be rendered permissible by the democratic process?[15] One type of answer focuses on the alleged instrumental benefits that democratic institutions deliver. These benefits might be epistemic or practical. Well-functioning democratic institutions, some argue, offer a better chance of arriving at sound decisions than any acceptable alternatives.[16] Others argue that democratic institutions are most likely to protect important rights and freedoms.[17]

These ideas will get a fuller hearing in chapter 4. For now, notice that these claims, even if true, do not—on their own—easily establish that legitimate injustice is possible. The fact that an institution has general instrumental value does not entail that everything done by that institution is morally permissible, nor that its officials have claims against harmful interference when they act unjustly. Your local college or university might be instrumentally

15. For a survey and critique of various arguments in support of a so-called democratic right to do wrong, see Øverland and Barry, "Do Democratic Societies Have a Right."

16. See, for example, Estlund, *Democratic Authority*; Landemore, *Democratic Reason*.

17. See, for example, Arneson, "Defending the Purely Instrumental Account."

valuable for its students, faculty, staff, and the surrounding community in all sorts of ways, but it would be bizarre to leap from that fact to the conclusion that university officials gain special permissions to commit injustice, or that they have rights against harmful interference when they do so.

Others emphasize the non-instrumental value of democratic institutions and decisions. In particular, democratic institutions have an egalitarian character that is held to be valuable independent of the content of the decisions those institutions produce.[18] The authority of democratic decisions is sometimes said to be grounded in this egalitarian feature.

We'll consider this view in greater depth in chapter 5. For now, we can note the difficulty in moving from the fact that decisions have been taken democratically to the conclusion that those decisions can be permissibly enforced when they are unjust, or that state officials have rights against harmful interference in enforcing unjust decisions. Many of us might agree that, when choosing amongst options that do not violate anyone's rights, there are reasons to make the choice democratically. But decisions to violate people's rights are different. Saying "we took a vote and the majority decided to violate your rights" does not seem like a sufficient justification. Perhaps there's more to be said about the special value of egalitarian decision-making. But absent some further argument, the proponent of Justice First can credibly insist that an appeal to democracy does not threaten any of the premises of the Impermissibility Argument or the Liability Argument.

What if Everyone Did That?

Consider a more pragmatic challenge. Imagine that most ordinary citizens become convinced of the truth of Justice First. They become convinced that state officials cannot permissibly enforce

18. For different versions of this view see, for example, Christiano, *Constitution of Equality*, 76; Valentini, "Justice, Disagreement," 178; Kolodny, "Rule Over None II," 317; Viehoff, "Democratic Equality," 340.

unjust laws, and those officials are, in principle, liable to harmful interference whenever they do so. Although citizens agree about Justice First, they continue to disagree sharply about all the issues citizens disagree about it in the world we know (affirmative action, abortion, redistributive taxation, immigration, etc.). The consequences of all this disagreement combined with widespread acceptance of Justice First could be disastrous. Governments will regularly be passing and attempting to enforce legislation that large portions of the public will view as unjust. If many citizens believe government officials enforcing such legislation are acting impermissibly and are liable to harmful interference, the government may find it very difficult to enforce much, if any, legislation. If state officials are constantly subject to interference and attack, many won't wish to serve in these roles, and those who do may be more likely to be the sort of people who enjoy violent conflict. Under these conditions, it might be very difficult to establish and maintain the rule of law and minimally just conditions. It's better, one might reasonably conclude, to live in a world where government officials can make mistakes; where they can permissibly enforce at least some unjust legislation and have claims against being harmfully interfered with. It's better, at the bar of justice, to live in such a world, rather than in a world where governments are unable to function effectively because state officials are constantly at risk of interference and attack from citizens acting under the influence of Justice First.

But this argument doesn't undermine the moral claims made by proponents of Justice First. All it shows is that it could be very bad if most people actually believed that Justice First is true. But moral claims cannot be false because bad consequences might follow if they were widely believed to be true.[19] The proponent of Justice First is not claiming that things would always go best if most people believed its central claims about permissibility and liability. The truth of these claims depends not on what would

19. Brennan offers this defense of Justice First in *When All Else Fails*, 107–15.

happen if many people believed them, but rather on whether there are sufficient reasons why government officials should have permissions and immunities with regard to injustice that ordinary people lack.

Summary

I have not canvassed all the possible challenges to Justice First, but hopefully I've made it clear how difficult it is to establish a disanalogy between government officials and ordinary persons when it comes to committing injustice. It's not plausible to suppose that the neighbors or the townspeople act permissibly—or have claims against harmful interference—when they threaten the rights of Albert and Bianca in Weed or Family Separation. And as we have seen, it's not easy to find a compelling argument why things should be different if we replace the neighbors and townspeople with government officials. The proponent of Justice First concludes that things are, in fact, no different. The puzzle of legitimate injustice is thus easily dismissed.

Rules, Rights, and Mistakes

We have just seen that the difficulties facing an opponent of Justice First are substantial. But in this, and the remaining sections of this chapter, I present three objections to Justice First that, taken collectively, provide good reasons to look elsewhere for a solution to the puzzle of legitimate injustice.

Consider the following story:

Mistaken Conviction: A murder has been committed. The police conduct a professional and thorough investigation. All the evidence and testimony that they uncover points clearly toward Clara as the murderer. Clara is arrested, charged, and stands trial. Her trial is conducted in an impeccably fair and impartial way. The jury is given clear access to all the evidence and Clara's defense attorney offers a robust defense of her client. But given the overwhelming evidence, the jury reasonably concludes that Clara is guilty. She is convicted and sentenced to twenty-five years in prison. Clara, however, is innocent of the crime: the evidence against her was cleverly manufactured and planted by the real murderer, though there was no reasonable way for the police, prosecutor, or jury to uncover this fact.

Clara is innocent and yet she is mistakenly sentenced to twenty-five years in prison. It is natural to conclude that she is the victim of a terrible injustice. She did nothing wrong, and so she is not liable to be incarcerated. By imprisoning her, state officials (and members of the jury too) have infringed Clara's rights. It is unjust for Clara to be in prison while the real murderer goes free.

But should we therefore conclude that the investigating officers, the jury, the prosecutor, the judge, the bailiff, and others have done something impermissible? Should we conclude that they are liable to harmful interference in defense of Clara's rights? I suspect many people will answer "no" to these questions. We can stipulate that at each stage of the process the relevant officials exercise due care, they do not exhibit any bias, they arrive at conclusions that are supported by the weight of the available evidence, and so on. Put differently, each state official involved in Clara's conviction and incarceration acts in a way that is *evidence-relative permissible*: that is, they do what morality apparently permits in light of the evidence available to them.[20] Indeed, given their official responsibilities, we can probably say something stronger: each does what they are *evidence-relative required* to do. It would be very strange to tell the judge, or one of the jurors, "You are acting impermissibly! Even though the evidence overwhelmingly points to Clara's guilt, you must acquit her!"

The proponent of Justice First faces a dilemma. On the one hand, they can insist, counterintuitively, that the jurors and state

20. For the distinction between evidence-relative, fact-relative, and belief-relative permissibility, see Parfit, *On What Matters, Volume 1*, 150–51.

officials have acted wrongly, and that they are liable to harmful interference in defense of Clara's rights. Alternatively, the proponent can say that Clara is not the victim of injustice—that her rights have not been infringed at all in this story. Let's consider each horn of the dilemma in a bit more detail.

The First Horn

Embracing the first horn of the dilemma might not seem so troubling. The proponent might say that while the jurors and state officials do act wrongly, they are epistemically excused and thus blameless. Once we recognize that this kind of blameless wrongdoing is possible, there's no difficulty with concluding the state officials and jurors do act wrongly.

I think there are at least two, closely related, problems with this proposal. First, insisting that the jurors and officials are blameless doesn't do much to defuse the counterintuitiveness of the position. The counterintuitiveness attaches to claims about what it would be right and wrong for the jurors and judge to do, rather than to their degree of culpability.

The deeper explanation as to why these claims are counterintuitive is grounded in a view of what morality can require of each of us. On one influential contractualist view, morality requires that we act in accordance with principles that no one can reasonably reject.[21] How to specify which principles are subject to reasonable rejection is notoriously controversial, but the process must depend, in part, on considering the relative costs and benefits that would accrue to different people under different proposals.

Consider two possible principles to regulate driving a car:

1) You cannot permissibly drive a car in a given instance unless you have taken various precautionary measures to ensure the safety of others (e.g., passed a driving test,

21. See Scanlon, *What We Owe.*

ensured your car meets various safety standards, adhered to all the rules of the road while driving).

2) You cannot permissibly drive a car in a given instance unless your belief that driving in this case will harm no one is correct.

There are compelling reasons to reject the second proposed principle. This principle is not directly action-guiding for epistemically limited agents like ourselves. We don't know, in any given instance, whether our decision to drive will harm others, since many things are not perfectly foreseeable (a patch of ice on the road, a child that darts into traffic, a sharp object that bursts a tire, etc.). If we do try to conform to the second proposed principle, we will thus have to adopt "second-best" strategies, but the rule itself offers no guidance about which strategies to adopt. One strategy might be extreme risk aversion: because we can never be certain our driving won't cause harm, we should never drive. But if everyone followed this strategy, we couldn't get all the tremendous benefits that come with the activity of driving. We could instead adopt much riskier second-best strategies of trying to comply with (2): for example, we could decide that whenever the chance our driving will harm others is less than 50 percent, we are permitted to drive. But widespread adoption of this strategy will also impose terrible costs. And if we don't specify which second-best strategy to adopt in an attempt to comply with (2), different people will predictably adopt different strategies, making other people's risk-imposing behavior less predictable (something that itself makes harm harder to avoid), and we may also end up distributing the risks of harm very unevenly across the population.[22]

By contrast, proposal (1) is something that is directly action-guiding; it doesn't require more evidence than agents typically possess. This makes its costs and benefits more readily measurable, it makes people's behavior more easily predictable, and if the

22. These points are made, in a slightly different context, in Bolinger, "Moral Grounds."

relevant regulations and rules of the road are well designed, the expected costs and benefits of the policy might be, *ex ante*, in each person's self-interest relative to most feasible alternatives. The upshot is that, in a range of scenarios, it's plausible to suppose that morality cannot demand that we "get it right" in the sense of acting in the way we ought to act if we were omniscient. Telling potential drivers, "Never drive if you will harm others," is indeterminate and too burdensome to serve as a moral directive for realistic agents.

We can extend this reasoning to the question of how to resolve uncertainty or disagreement about moral rights.[23] A principle directing people to "get it right" in cases of uncertainty or disagreement about moral rights may be indeterminate under realistic conditions, and it may create unjustifiable burdens as a result. It may be that the most we can reasonably require of anyone—at least in some cases where there's uncertainty or disagreement about moral rights—is that they accept as authoritative a fair legal resolution of the uncertainty/disagreement, rather than follow their own judgment. A principle directing jurors, prosecutors, judges, and others simply to "convict only the guilty" is one that they cannot directly operationalize, and as a result such a principle is likely to create many burdens that cannot be justified when compared to the alternative of following a series of well-designed rules for the criminal law. If that's true, the jurors, the prosecutor, the judge, and other officials do not act wrongly in cases like Mistaken Conviction.

Criminal trials are, of course, not the only domain where this reasoning might apply. A similar argument might apply in cases where citizens or legislators conscientiously do their best to enact just legislation, but sometimes err and mistakenly enact unjust legislation. In some of these cases it may be that we cannot reasonably demand citizens and legislators simply follow the directive to "get it right." It may be that the most we can reasonably demand is

23. For a distinctive recent view about how to resolve uncertainty about moral rights, see Stone, "Putting Freedom of Contract."

that others accept, and act in conformity with, the results of a legislative resolution.

The argument that I've just sketched is not uncontroversial. Among other things, it depends on a contractualist framework that some reject, and which faces various objections of its own. It also depends on claims about the moral significance of disagreement that I did not spell out (though we'll discuss these claims further in chapters 5 and 6). But it does provide a deeper explanation for the commonsense intuition that the jurors, the prosecutor, the judge, and others need not have done anything wrong in Mistaken Conviction. It explains why, at least sometimes, when someone sincerely says, "I exercised all due care and followed all the appropriate procedures/precautions," this is a justification, and not merely an excuse, even when their actions are, from an omniscient point of view, a mistake.

The Second Horn

The proponent of Justice First might thus opt for the second horn of the dilemma, concluding that Clara suffers no injustice in Mistaken Conviction and therefore the jurors and state officials act permissibly. The proponent might insist that Clara does not have a moral right against being convicted. What she has instead is a right to a fair trial including competent legal representation, a right to appeal against the result, a right against mistreatment while incarcerated, a right against disproportionate criminal punishment, and so on. But in Mistaken Conviction the duties that correlate with all these rights are fulfilled—no one infringes any of these claims. As a result, Clara is not treated unjustly. On this view what happens to Clara is, of course, a tragedy, but it's not an injustice.

This conclusion, however, is difficult to accept. Clara being incarcerated is not like tragedies that result from brute bad luck. Clara did not suffer an accident, nor was she diagnosed with some serious disease. Other people made a series of deliberate choices, for which they are responsible, that caused her to be incarcerated.

Suppose that, several years into serving her sentence, it is discovered that Clara is innocent of the crime. Wouldn't we think that Clara is entitled to compensation for the years she was mistakenly incarcerated? But if her rights were not infringed—if she was not wronged by being incarcerated—why should she be entitled to any compensation? If we want to explain Clara's entitlement to compensation, it seems we ought to concede that her rights were infringed.

There's a deeper explanation of the judgment that Clara's rights have been infringed. Our moral rights are important in large part because they provide each of us with a measure of control over our own lives. Your rights give you a sphere where your own choices, rather than the choices of others, are typically decisive. This is better achieved when right-holders have effective control over whether or not they render themselves liable to various forms of harm and interference against which persons typically have claims. You have this kind of control when the loss or forfeiture of your rights depends on your own voluntary choices (e.g., the decision to commit a crime). But we don't have this kind of control if retaining rights is not dependent on our own choices, but is rather contingent upon what others believe we have done. Suppose the question arises as to whether you still own the blue Honda Civic that you bought last year, or whether you've sold the ownership rights to your neighbor Dan. For you, and for right-holders generally, it makes much more sense for the answer to this question to depend on choices that you've actually made, as opposed to reasonable beliefs that others might have formed. This, I submit, is part of the explanation for the commonsense view that Clara is the victim of an injustice, and not merely misfortune, in Mistaken Conviction.

How can this line of thought be reconciled with the argument that we cannot reasonably demand that others simply "get it right," when this would require omniscience? There are several different options, but here is one. We don't always have claim rights that others should simply "get it right." In some cases, where there is uncertainty or disagreement about first-order moral rights, the most we can reasonably demand of others is that they exercise due care, and follow any appropriate, fair adjudicative procedures. But when others actually treat us as if we have done something wrong—as if we have rendered ourselves liable to defensive harm or liable to criminal punishment—they must "get it right" on pain of infringing our moral rights.[24] Having the effective control to avoid criminal liability and liability to defensive harm is particularly important given the severity of the harms and the loss of moral and legal standing. The importance of retaining this control may explain why Clara's rights really are infringed, even if the jurors and state officials cannot be said to have acted impermissibly, since they did all that could be reasonably demanded of them.

But notice that proponents of Justice First cannot help themselves to this proposal without abandoning the substantive core of their position. The proposal allows for the possibility of permissible injustice, but what renders the injustice permissible is the fact that state officials are complying with specific legal procedures and we cannot reasonably demand that they do otherwise. In sum, the proponent of Justice First faces an awkward dilemma in cases like Mistaken Conviction. Either they must insist the jurors and other officials act impermissibly, or else they must insist that Clara is not the victim of injustice.

Attacking State Officials

Justice First tells us that state officials are no different from ordinary citizens when it comes to committing injustice. If we set aside lesser-evil justifications, ordinary citizens typically act impermissibly if they commit an injustice and they lack moral rights against necessary and proportionate defensive harm. Think about the neighbors and the townspeople in Weed and Family Separation.

---

24. I defend a particular version of this idea with regard to liability to defensive harm in Quong, *Morality of Defensive Force*, chs. 2 and 6.

If, for example, the only way for Albert to get the neighbors to leave him and his property unharmed was to punch one of the neighbors, fracturing a rib, I think Albert would be permitted to do so. He would be defending his rights against a wrongful threat using necessary and proportionate force. Suppose the only way for Bianca to prevent the townspeople from wrongfully detaining her in their "camp" is to shoot one of them in the foot: she would surely be permitted to do this. Like Albert, she would only be using necessary and proportionate force to defend her rights.

If state officials are no different from ordinary citizens, then we may also permissibly use defensive violence against those officials when they attempt to enforce unjust laws and policies. Justice First thus appears to tell us that we may harm, even kill, government officials who enforce democratically authorized, but unjust, legislation. If the tax authorities try to take an unjust share of your wealth, you can resist, with force if necessary. Police officers who try to enforce an unjust law restricting speech by shutting down a Nazi march are, in principle, liable to be attacked to defend the Nazis' rights of free speech. If the government passes unjust abortion legislation, state officials enforcing the law are liable to be harmed, or even killed. And so on.

These conclusions are difficult to accept. Most of us do not believe that state officials—acting in good faith and executing democratically enacted legislation that doesn't contravene widely accepted human rights—are liable to violent attack even when the laws they enforce are unjust. The problem is not that allowing such conduct would have very bad consequences, though it might. It is rather that the moral claim appears to be false.

In response to this objection, the proponent of Justice First has two main avenues. First, they can insist that the moral claim about officials' liability to defensive harm is true—indeed they may argue it is one of the central and appealing features of their view. Contrary to popular belief, government officials shouldn't be immune to defensive harm when they threaten people's rights. Of course, most people have been conditioned to accept their government's authority and to believe government officials have a special immunity to do things ordinary people cannot. But this commonsense belief is easily debunked—it's very much in the interests of governments and state officials that this belief be widely accepted, and they often work hard to ridicule and violently suppress those who question it. We thus have good reasons to distrust ordinary beliefs about this issue.

Although there is some merit to this response, it's inadequate. Discomfort with the idea that state officials are liable to be attacked or even killed when they attempt to enforce unjust laws cannot be explained away as nothing more than the result of government indoctrination. As we saw when considering the Mistaken Conviction example, there are deeper theoretical reasons to suspect that state officials sometimes do not act wrongly, even when they infringe the rights of citizens. State officials, at least in constitutional democracies, are tasked with fulfilling morally important roles. When they execute those roles in good faith, we have reason to be skeptical that they should be liable to attack in the same way as the neighbors or townspeople are in our other examples. Unlike the neighbors or townspeople, they have not simply appropriated political power for themselves. Unlike the neighbors or townspeople, they act on behalf of the entire political community. Unlike the neighbors and the townspeople, they are acting within the constraints of the law. These differences seem, at least prima facie, to be morally significant. At the very least, it's not obvious that people who act in this latter way are equally liable to harmful interference as those who unilaterally commit injustice outside the bounds of the law.

It is noteworthy that even proponents of Justice First seem uncomfortable with the implications of their view regarding the liability of government officials to defensive attack. Brennan, for example, sometimes relies on examples where state officials are not simply enforcing unjust legislation, but are rather acting outside the bounds of the law (e.g., police shooting a driver who poses no threat, or police viciously beating a drunk driver who has already been apprehended and subdued).[25] It is much easier to accept the view that police officers using unnecessary and illegal violence are liable to harm than it is to believe that government agents acting competently, in good faith, and within the bounds of the law, are liable to be harmed or killed when the laws they enforce are unjust.

There is, however, another way for proponents of Justice First to respond. There is an ongoing debate about the necessary and sufficient conditions for liability to defensive harm. On one account, culpability is a necessary condition for liability to defensive harm.[26] Those who threaten the rights of others but are entirely excused for doing so—for example, because they are unavoidably ignorant that they pose an unjust threat, or perhaps because they are temporarily mentally incompetent—are not liable to defensive attack. If this account is correct, then competent state officials acting in good faith might frequently not be liable to attack, since they might be unavoidably ignorant that they pose unjust threats in fulfilling their roles. This conclusion is consistent with Justice First, since it doesn't grant state officials any special, or unique, immunity; it rather offers them immunity from attack on the very same basis that anyone else is immune: namely, when you are fully excused for posing a wrongful threat. We have thus apparently found a way to affirm Justice First while avoiding some of the most counterintuitive implications of the view.

This strategy, however, faces serious problems. The idea that culpability is necessary for liability to defensive harm is not widely endorsed, and for good reasons.[27] Suppose that Albert has been convincingly duped into believing his neighbor is about to kill him and so prepares to kill his neighbor in "self-defense," but that as a

25. These examples appear throughout Brennan, *When All Else Fails*. Examples where government officials competently and legally enforce unjust laws are also considered.

26. For a version of this account see, for example, Ferzan, "Culpable Aggression."

27. For criticisms of culpability as a necessary condition of liability see, for example, McMahan, "Basis of Moral Liability"; Quong, *Morality of Defensive Force*, 23–25.

matter of fact his neighbor poses no threat at all. If culpability is a necessary condition for liability then, counterintuitively, Albert isn't liable to defensive harm and a third party cannot seriously harm Albert to stop him from killing his neighbor. Unlike criminal liability, the purpose of defensive harm is not retributive, but only to protect the rights of another. When that is the goal—as it is in the case of tort liability—we generally don't require a culpability standard. Most philosophers have concluded that there is no compelling reason why liability to defensive harm should be different in this respect.

Even if we set these worries aside, embracing the claim that culpability is necessary for liability threatens to deprive Justice First of much of its initial appeal. If state officials are immune from interference whenever they are fully excused for their actions, Justice First will sometimes be unable to explain why anyone can harmfully interfere with state officials, even when those officials enforce egregiously unjust laws or make grave errors. Those state officials may non-culpably believe that they do nothing wrong so long as they do their duty and the laws they enforce fall within constitutional limits.

Dealing with Disagreement

The most serious problem with Justice First, however, is its silence concerning one of the most central and intractable features of our political life: disagreement. Every modern political community is characterized by an enormous degree of political disagreement. We disagree about so very much: redistributive taxation, free speech and "cancel culture," gun regulation, abortion, immigration, environmental regulation, the rights of felons, the rights of children, educational policy, and thousands of other topics. Some (though, of course, not all) of these disagreements are competent, good-faith disagreements. By that I mean that the participants who hold opposing views are reasonably well informed, thoughtful, sincerely motivated to do what is right, and the policy positions they advance are grounded in widely accepted values or principles. History teaches us that these disagreements are not going away—they seem to be a permanent feature of life in any sufficiently free society. One of the most central, enduring questions in politics is what we should do about this disagreement. Are there principles of justice that regulate how such disagreements ought to be resolved? Any successful account of political morality must address this question.

What do proponents of Justice First say in answer to this question? Their main response is that, insofar as political disagreement reflects the fact that some people hold mistaken views about justice, then to cater to, or respect, those who hold false views is to compromise with injustice.[28] When we design our institutions or actions to take into account that some people will be guided by false beliefs about justice, we are departing from what justice in fact requires merely to avoid even worse outcomes. This should be acknowledged for what it is: a lesser-evil justification. But, say the proponents of Justice First, we should only cater to injustice if we have to. If the people with the mistaken, unjust views can be tricked, overcome, or otherwise defeated without compromising what justice requires, then you shouldn't compromise.

The implications of this position are extraordinarily counterintuitive. It entails that there's nothing wrong, in principle, with tampering with election results, or hacking into people's bank accounts and taking money, so long as doing so better promotes what justice truly requires and won't have sufficiently bad consequences. It entails that we are always, in principle, permitted to ignore legal and other conventional rules when those rules conflict with the true requirements of justice, even when the legal or other conventional rules represent our community's attempt to resolve competent, good-faith disagreement about the requirements of justice.

28. See, for example, Brennan, *When All Else Fails*, 197–205; Wellman, "Space Between."

This ignores a fairly obvious possibility: there might be procedural or second-order principles of justice that regulate how we ought to resolve certain disagreements about first-order political questions. Our political rights—to vote, run for elected office, and otherwise participate in the democratic process—are claims of justice. We have claims of justice to participate on roughly equal terms with others in the resolution of (at least many of) our first-order disagreements about politics. Justice First apparently insists that the scope of these political rights is vastly narrower than most of us believe. Most of us believe that your rights to vote and run for elected office are not contingent on not making any mistakes about the requirements of justice.

Suppose, for example, candidates A and B disagree about health care policy, which is the central issue in the current election. Both have adopted thoughtful, well-reasoned proposals, but as a matter of fact, A's proposal is just and B's proposal is unjust. In all other respects their policy positions are equivalently acceptable from the standpoint of justice. Justice First—at least under the current interpretation—tells us that the scope of B's right to run for office does not extend to cover enacting her unjust health care plan, and ordinary citizens do not have protected claim rights to vote for B, given that B's central policy plank is unjust. No rights would be infringed, for example, if a third party tampered with the election results to prevent many people's votes for B from being counted. Only candidates and voters who exercise their political power in ways consistent with the true requirements of justice are acting in ways protected by moral rights.

This is a very revisionist account of our political rights. Most of us believe our rights to vote and run for office protect us from harmful interference even when we make mistakes—even if we vote for the candidate who will implement unjust policies or support unjust ballot initiatives. It does not seem plausible to claim that whenever we disagree about how political power should be justly exercised, the just resolution to these disagreements turns only on who is correct—that there is no independent principle of justice concerning the procedural resolution of the disagreement.

Suppose the proponent of Justice First concedes that there are independent principles of justice that regulate the distribution of political power. They accept that our claims to participate in the democratic process on equal terms with others are not conditional (at least within limits) on exercising that power correctly. Making this concession avoids one set of problems, but it threatens to undermine the central claims of Justice First. If there are principles of justice that allocate rights to vote and run for elected office even when those rights are exercised to promote unjust policies, then we have conflicting claims of justice. Persons' political rights to participate in the democratic process on roughly equal terms will sometimes yield results that conflict with their substantive rights (e.g., to grow and ingest intoxicants, or to receive a certain share of society's resources, or to travel freely across political borders). What should we do about such conflicts?

We can no longer simply assert, with proponents of Justice First, that it is impermissible to commit injustice and that all of us, including government officials, lack claims against harmful interference when we do so. Arguments are required to establish how to handle the conflicting claims of justice. But without such arguments in hand, there's no reason to suppose that it's impermissible to respect the outcomes of the democratic process rather than subvert those results in order to protect other, substantive claims of justice. After all, whatever happens in these cases, some rights will be infringed. A presumption against injustice does nothing to settle which claims of justice are those that ought to take priority in cases of conflict, and thus it does nothing to support the conclusions that government officials cannot permissibly enforce unjust laws, nor possess rights against harmful interference when they do so.

In sum, competent, good-faith disagreement is a pervasive and intractable feature of our political life. But such disagreement poses serious problems for Justice First. On the one hand, proponents of Justice First can insist disagreement is largely irrelevant—in particular, there are no principles of justice that directly regulate how disagreements are to be resolved. But this entails that our political rights to vote and run for elected office are far narrower in scope than is widely assumed—that there are no protected rights to make errors about justice in political life. On the other hand, proponents of Justice First might concede there are separate principles of justice regulating the distribution of political power, and these principles grant rights to participate in the political process even when we make mistakes about justice. But this concession undermines the core arguments that support Justice First, leaving us without sufficient reason to accept its conclusions.

Conclusion

Justice First offers a clear and sometimes compelling resolution to the puzzle of legitimate injustice. It dismisses the puzzle by rejecting the idea that government officials get a free pass to commit injustice. Justice First is the right place to start thinking about the apparent tension between justice and legitimacy. It provides a much needed dose of skepticism regarding many views in political philosophy concerning the scope of state officials' moral permissions and immunities. But although it's a good place to start thinking about our puzzle, I don't think it's the right place to stop. Justice First requires the adoption of views about permissibility, liability, and political disagreement that are, cumulatively, extraordinarily difficult to accept. The intuitive and theoretical costs of accepting such views are steep enough to make it worth searching for alternative resolutions to our puzzle.

3

Freedom, Law, and Justice

THE PREVIOUS chapter examined a view that I dubbed Justice First. Proponents of this view, as the name suggests, deny the existence of legitimate injustice. They deny, that is, that state officials typically act permissibly in enforcing unjust laws, and they deny that state officials typically have claim rights against harmful interference when they enforce unjust laws. The view has obvious appeal for those of us who believe that justice is of paramount importance—that it is the first virtue of social institutions. But despite its appeal, Justice First flounders because it seems to ignore or quickly dismiss one of the most central and intractable facts of political life: there is no widespread agreement about the specific requirements of justice. How can justice be prioritized if we disagree so deeply about what it requires?

In this chapter I turn to consider a view that retains the ironclad commitment to the priority of justice, while taking disagreement about the content of justice to be one of the defining problems of political life. The view originates in the political and legal philosophy of Immanuel Kant.[1] Although Kant's ethical theory is better known, in recent decades there has been a surge of excellent work from philosophers inspired by Kant's views about politics and law. Japa Pallikkathayil, Arthur Ripstein, Anna Stilz, and Ernest Weinrib (to name only a few) have developed Kantian theories that

1. Kant, *Metaphysics of Morals*.

offer a distinctive picture of justice and the law.[2] The central claim is that there is a constitutive relationship between the coercive legal power of the state and the rights to which each of us are entitled as a matter of justice. On the Kantian view, it is only via the establishment of a legitimate legal order that justice is possible. Justice is not something that competes or conflicts with the importance of legitimate legal procedures, nor are these procedures mere instruments through which we might hope to better realize independent standards of justice. Rather, a legitimate legal and political authority renders determinate the otherwise indeterminate requirements of justice, thus making just relations between persons possible.

This Kantian picture has many attractions, including the apparent capacity to dispel the puzzle of legitimate injustice. That puzzle, as a reminder, centers on the following three claims:

1) "Justice is the first virtue of social institutions, as truth is of systems of thought. A theory however elegant and economical must be rejected or revised if it is untrue; likewise laws and institutions no matter how efficient and well-arranged must be reformed or abolished if they are unjust."[3]

2) Some ordinary laws in liberal democratic societies are unjust.

3) Many of these laws can be legitimate: that is, state officials act permissibly in enforcing these laws and they have rights against harmful interference while enforcing them.

Insofar as the laws are issued by a legitimate public authority, there is no puzzle, on the Kantian view, because such laws cannot be unjust. Therefore, the second claim that constitutes the puzzle is

2. See, for example, Pallikkathayil, "Deriving Morality; Pallikkathayil, "Neither Perfectionism"; Ripstein, "Authority and Coercion."; Ripstein, *Force and Freedom*; Stilz, *Liberal Loyalty*; Weinrib, *Idea of Private Law*.

3. Rawls, *Theory of Justice*, 3.

false. While such laws may be aptly criticized on various grounds—for example, as inefficient, unfair, or unnecessary—they cannot be unjust, because they constitute our rights and duties with regard to one another, thus defining what justice requires of us.

The chapter proceeds as follows. I begin by outlining the central problem of political life on the Kantian view. The core problem is generated by two facts: the indeterminacy of justice and the absence, in the state of nature, of a mechanism of resolving this indeterminacy in a manner consistent with each person's right to independence. The only solution to this problem, on the Kantian view, is the creation of a legitimate public authority that renders our rights determinate and assures us that our rights will be respected. This solution also apparently enables the Kantian view to resolve the puzzle of legitimate injustice by rejecting the second claim. Although the Kantian view is in many respects compelling, I argue that the account faces a serious dilemma. The Kantian can insist that the substantive requirements of justice are largely indeterminate. But this is difficult to reconcile with many of our considered convictions and social practices—in particular, with how most of us conceptualize, at least, many important political disagreements. To avoid this difficulty, the Kantian might retreat, conceding that at least some important questions about justice have determinate answers. But this creates a new dilemma. The Kantian must either insist, implausibly, that the unilateral imposition of justice remains inconsistent with equal freedom even in cases where justice is determinate, or else she must concede that such unilateral imposition of determinate requirements is consistent with each person's right to independence, departing from the way Kantians understand the state's legitimate authority.

A Kantian Problem

For Kant, our right to external freedom—freedom from the constraints of the choices of others—is the sole innate right. "There is only one innate right," says Kant, "freedom (independence from being constrained by another's choice), insofar as it can coexist with the freedom of every other in accordance with a universal law."[4] But what, more precisely, is entailed by this right to external freedom?[5] Freedom, in Kant's sense, requires there to be some domain where you, rather than any other person, have the authority to determine what shall occur. You have this freedom with regard to your body, for example, when your choices, rather than anyone else's, settle for what ends or purposes your body may be used. Slavery is the paradigm example of unfreedom, since there is no domain where the slave's choices are sovereign. To be free is thus to have rightful authority over some part of the world—your means. You may use your means however you see fit, provided that you do not encroach on the means of others. Encroaching on another person's means is to threaten that person's independence. This can be done in three ways: by depriving a person of his means, by forcing a person to pursue ends he does not share, or by using another person's means without consent.[6] Each constitutes an interference with independence, because in each case one person has subjected the other to his will.

On the Kantian account, freedom is a social relation between persons, and not a matter of individual autonomy. Whether you are a free is not a question of whether you have deliberated in an appropriate manner, nor whether you are the author, or at least part author, of your own choices. Someone who would not be considered autonomous by the lights of much contemporary philosophy—an unreflective agent who does not carefully weigh the reasons for his actions and tends to follow inherited traditions without much thought—can be externally free in Kant's sense so long as there is a secure domain where his choices, rather than anyone else's, are decisive in determining what occurs.

4. Kant, *Metaphysics of Morals*, 30.
5. My presentation of the Kantian account in this section and the next is indebted to the more detailed works cited in note 2 above.
6. For discussion, see Ripstein, "Authority and Coercion," 11–22.

Because external freedom is a social relation, it is a zero-sum political value. Increasing one person's external freedom necessarily restricts someone else's. If we increase the domain where A's choices settle what will occur, we have necessarily limited the available means where B's choices could be sovereign. Freedom is a matter of assigning rights of control over the external world. Because the external world is finite, any increase in one person's rights constitutes a decrease for at least someone else.

This puts the Kantian account at odds with at least a good deal of liberal political philosophy, where it's often assumed that there is a "presumption" in favor of liberty.[7] On this alternative picture, freedom is purely a matter of non-interference. The baseline normative position is that interference is unjustified—and thus a sufficiently compelling justification must always be provided for the interference to be permissible. This picture of freedom is inconsistent with the Kantian view. The mere absence of interference is not freedom on the Kantian view, since that absence does not ensure that one's choices are sovereign. The benevolent master who chooses not to interfere with his slave does not render his slave free on the Kantian account.[8]

The presumption in favor of liberty is also inconsistent with the Kantian view because it assumes that coercion or interference is always a presumptive threat to freedom. On the Kantian account, by contrast, there can be no general presumption against coercion. There is only a presumption against coercion that is unilateral. Ensuring freedom for everyone in fact requires the enforcement of people's rights. When a person's conclusive rights are protected via the use of threats or force, there's no presumption against this conduct that needs to be overcome.

---

7. Ripstein emphasizes this contrast in "Authority and Coercion."

8. In this respect, as well as several others, there is a good deal of overlap between the Kantian account of freedom-as-independence and the republican account of freedom-as-non-domination. For instructive critical discussion that considers these views together, see Kolodny, "Being Under the Power."

In sum, freedom in the Kantian sense requires that each person be assured of a secure domain where her choices, rather than anyone else's, are decisive in settling what may rightfully be done with that part of the world. Only when each of us has such a domain do we have freedom-as-independence—the freedom to set our own ends independent from the wills or needs of others.

We now come to the central problem. Freedom in the sense just described evidently requires a determinate allocation of rights over our bodies and the rest of the external world. But the Kantian account of freedom-as-independence is very abstract—it doesn't entail any particular allocation of rights over the external world. To be sure, it excludes some distributions of rights. For example, any allocation that denies some people any rights at all, or which affords some people rights so meagre that they are unable to set any ends without the permission of others, is inconsistent with freedom-as-independence. But there are many different ways of specifying persons' moral rights that will be consistent with freedom-as-independence. Freedom in Kant's sense is therefore consistent with a vast array of conflicting views about, among other things, what specific rights and liberties people possess, the distribution of income and wealth, and many of the rules of tort and contract law. The concept of independence cannot tell us, for example, the precise contours of our rights to free speech, or whether liability in tort law should sometimes be strict, or what tax rates should be for people with different levels of income and wealth, or what exactly reasonable care requires in tort. Freedom-as-independence is simply indeterminate with regard to a vast number of substantive questions about how rights over the world ought to be allocated. This indeterminacy must be resolved in order to realize freedom-as-independence; in order for just relations between persons to exist.

In a state of nature—a condition without an established legal order—each person will have their own views about justice; about the allocation of moral rights over the world. There will inevitably be clashes when parties disagree about which parts of the world rightfully belong to whom. Although these disagreements may become violent, and are sub-optimal with regard to people's interests or welfare, neither of those facts are the fundamental problem for the Kantian. The fundamental problem is rather that the innate right to external freedom is indeterminate, and unless it can be rendered determinate just relations between persons are impossible. Without rights over determinate parts of the world that are enforced by a competent authority, no one is independent—no one has a secure domain to set and pursue their ends free from the judgment or needs of others.[9]

But in the state of nature there's no way—consistent with the independence of persons—to render the requirements of justice determinate. Each has his or her own views about justice, and any attempt by one to enforce those views on others constitutes the unilateral imposition of that person's will on others, contrary to their independence.[10] There can be no reciprocal or mutual independence if some are simply forced to accept the judgments of others. But without a regime of determinate rights that is competently enforced, there can also be no independence. As Kant says, this "would be a state *devoid of justice (status iustitia vacuus)*, in which when rights are *in dispute (ius controversum)*, there would be no judge competent to render a verdict having rightful force."[11] This is the problem from which there is no escape in the state of nature.

A Kantian Solution

The Kantian solution to this problem—indeed, the only solution—is to have a legitimate public authority.

One influential tradition in political philosophy suggests that the state gains its rightful or legitimate authority via a

---

9. As Kant puts it, in the state of nature we could have merely "provisionally rightful" possession of things, but this falls short of a legitimate, conclusive right. Kant, *Metaphysics of Morals*, 51–52.

10. Kant, *Metaphysics of Morals*, 45.

11. Kant, *Metaphysics of Morals*, 90.

(hypothetical) transfer of moral rights from persons in the state of nature. People notionally choose to transfer the natural rights that they possess in the state of nature to gain the security and advantages of an organized political community. On this view people transfer to the state, among other things, their natural rights to defense and enforcement. On the Kantian approach, by contrast, conclusive rights do not exist in the state of nature, and so no transfer of such rights to the state is possible.

Without a story about rights being transferred from persons to the state, how does the state possess the right to rule? In particular, how does the state avoid the problem of unilateral imposition? The answer is, the rule of law. Private persons in the state of nature, no matter how well-meaning, can only ever act on their own private judgments. When they attempt to enforce what they take to be the requirements of justice, this is necessarily a unilateral imposition because it reflects the will or judgment of a private party. But the rule of law constitutes a different form of determination and enforcement. A regime governed by the rule of law is one where authority ultimately resides in laws, institutions, and offices, and not with particular persons.[12] Provided the laws satisfy certain constraints (more on this below), they do not reflect anyone's unilateral judgment; they instead reflect a universal or omnilateral will. The exercise of legitimate public authority is omnilateral both because it is exercised on behalf the entire polity, rather than on behalf of any particular person, and because power is not exercised in order to promote particular ends or purposes, but rather to create the formal conditions of innate right, conditions that make it possible for people to be independent and set their own ends.[13] These two senses in which the state's authority is omnilateral are closely related, and it's worth pausing to briefly elaborate on them.

Legitimate political authority must be consistent with what Kant calls the "original contract." The original contract refers

12. Kant, *Metaphysics of Morals*, 89–91.
13. Ripstein, *Force and Freedom*, 196.

not to any actual historical agreement, but rather to general terms to which all persons subject to political authority could rationally consent or will. Given the abstract nature of freedom-as-independence, the original contract will not make determinate prescriptions about the specific laws or institutions that must be created. Rather, it sets a constraint or limit on the exercise of the state's legitimate authority. It precludes any laws or institutions to which "a whole people could not *possibly* agree."[14] Institutions that permit slavery or hereditary legal privileges are precluded by this test, as are exercises of power that deprive some citizens of the opportunity to acquire any means of their own. The original contract also requires a particular form of republican self-government, with an appropriate separation of powers between the legislative, executive, and judicial branches.[15] When the state exercises its power in a manner consistent with the original con-tract, it acts on behalf of the entire community. It exercises its power in an omnilateral, rather than a unilateral, way.

If legitimate exercises of political power must be omnilateral in this sense, it follows that there is only one fundamental purpose for which political power can be legitimately exercised: to create and sustain the conditions required for each person's right to freedom-as-independence. This purpose is one that we all share, and it grounds the state's authority to legislate, to execute law, and to adju-dicate legal disputes. By performing these functions, the state re-solves the problems of indeterminacy and lack of assurance that were intractable in the state of nature. It provides each person with a set of determinate rights over their bodies and other parts of the world, which then enable each of us to be genuinely independent.

On the Kantian account there is no other legitimate purpose for which the state may exercise its power. It cannot exercise power to pursue particular ends or objectives. It cannot, for ex-ample, pursue the goal of religious salvation, or the promotion of

14. Kant, "On the Common Saying," 79.
15. Ripstein, *Force and Freedom*, 203.

hedonic pleasure, or set itself any other ends that are irrelevant to securing the mutual independence of persons.[16] If the state pursued such goals, it would no longer be acting on behalf of everyone, because these are not goals that all rational persons must share. Such exercises of power are unilateral, and thus inconsistent with mutual or reciprocal independence.

This view of legitimate political authority represents a striking departure from several ideas that have been mostly dominant in contemporary political philosophy. First, as I noted above, many claim that freedom consists in the absence of interference by others. With this notion of freedom in hand, they hold that there is a presumption in favor of liberty—it is always interference or coercion that stands in need of special justification—the moral default is that coercion is wrongful. This combination of views places a substantial burden on the justification of political authority. States clearly engage in massive amounts of coercion and interference with persons' choices, and so there's a strong presumption against their existence. The most common strategy for explaining how, despite this presumption, states can nevertheless be legitimate appeals to their instrumental value. States are presented as instruments for realizing certain morally important goals or interests, such as peace, security, and well-being.

Kantians reject each one of these ideas. First, freedom for the Kantian is not the mere absence of interference. It is having a secure domain where your choices, rather than anyone else's choices, determine what will occur. There is thus no moral presumption in favor of non-interference. We cannot increase the total amount of Kantian freedom by engaging in less interference. Second, freedom-as-independence isn't possible without determinate and enforceable moral rights, and so coercion is not a presumptive threat to freedom. Legitimate coercion is rather a constitutive feature of realizing reciprocal or mutual freedom. Thus, for the

---

16. Kant, "On the Common Saying," 80. Also see, for example, Pallikkathayil, "Neither Perfectionism."

Kantian, the state isn't a necessary evil, whose existence is justified in instrumental terms. Rather, the state constitutes just relations between persons by rendering our moral rights determinate and enforceable.

The Absence of Legitimate Injustice

The Kantian picture of political philosophy has a number of appealing features. To begin with, it acknowledges a truth—the indeterminacy of justice—that a great deal of work in analytic philosophy fails to reckon with. Reflection on our intractable disagreements about justice, and also the fact that many different legal regimes exist that appear to have an equal claim to be just, gives us some reason to think the Kantian view is correct. Justice is largely indeterminate in the absence of a legitimate legal regime which can specify rights over property, contract, tort, and much else.

The Kantian view also provides a way of vindicating the thought that political authority is not a necessary evil, but rather a constitutive element of what it is to live on just terms with others. On another influential view, the fundamental problem with the state of nature is that it's not in our self-interest to live in such a condition; because of the lack of a centralized authority we won't be safe and it will be difficult to advance our well-being effectively. The Kantian conception provides us with a way to explain what is problematic about the state of nature without appealing to our self-interest. On the Kantian picture, we have a moral duty to leave the state of nature because no one can be free in such a condition. We can only realize justice by departing from such a condition.

Finally, and most importantly for present purposes, the Kantian account promises to eliminate the puzzle of legitimate injustice. The puzzle arises, recall, insofar as we are inclined to affirm all three of the following claims:

1) "Justice is the first virtue of social institutions, as truth is of systems of thought. A theory however elegant and

economical must be rejected or revised if it is untrue; likewise laws and institutions no matter how efficient and well-arranged must be reformed or abolished if they are unjust."[17]

2) Some ordinary laws in liberal democratic societies are unjust.

3) Many of these laws can be legitimate: that is, state officials act permissibly in enforcing these laws and they have rights against harmful interference while enforcing them.

On the Kantian account, justice is indeterminate in the absence of a rightful public authority. There are no conclusive moral rights, and thus no claims of justice, in the state of nature. It is only via the establishment of a legitimate authority and the rule of law that it's possible to resolve this indeterminacy. The laws of a legitimate state give determinate content to our moral rights—they settle what rights we possess and what duties we owe one another as a matter of justice. Thus, the Kantian resolves the puzzle of legitimate injustice by denying the second claim. The ordinary laws of a liberal democratic society cannot be unjust. As Kant says, "The legislative authority can belong only to the united will of the people. For since all right is to proceed from it, it *cannot* do anyone wrong by its law."[18]

To claim otherwise assumes that there are determinate moral rights or claims of justice that exist in the absence of any rightful authority, and against which the laws passed by a rightful authority can be assessed. But on the Kantian view, there are no determinate pre-institutional claims of justice. Thus, there's no puzzle to be resolved. The laws of a legitimate state cannot be unjust, because those laws constitute the requirements of justice.

17. Rawls, *Theory of Justice*, 3.

18. Kant, *Metaphysics of Morals*, 91. Elsewhere, Kant says that public law "is the act of a public will, from which all right proceeds and which must not therefore be able to do an injustice to anyone." This is true, according to Kant, because the public will cannot commit an injustice against itself, in the same way as an individual person cannot commit an injustice against herself. Kant, "On the Common Saying," 77.

The Kantian position doesn't entail that the laws of a legitimate state are immune from criticism. Laws can aptly be criticized as unfair, inefficient, too blunt, or on any number of other grounds. We thus might often have perfectly good reasons to protest laws and seek to reform them. But since the law determines our rights and duties, these reasons cannot aptly be characterized by complaints of injustice.[19]

Of course, some political regimes do commit injustice understood in Kantian terms. They enact and enforce legislation that is inconsistent with the sole principle of innate right: the independence of persons. A regime might, for example, permit involuntary slavery, or prevent some citizens from acquiring any property of their own. Such regimes leave their subjects in a situation of unilateral force. In failing to respect subjects' independence, they simply force subjects to do certain things. The Kantian term for such a state of affairs is *barbarism*.[20] Although such unilateral imposition of force may be highly organized, and may superficially resemble a legal regime in many ways, on the Kantian picture this is simply another version of the state of nature. There is no rightful rule of law and thus no omnilateral will—there is just an organized unilateral exercise of power.[21] Such exercises of power cannot be instances of legitimate injustice, because they aren't legitimate. As Ripstein puts it, "The use of force is only rightful provided that it

19. Kant also insists that "all resistance" against a rightful legislative authority is "the greatest and most punishable crime in a commonwealth, for it destroys its very foundations." The people existing in a civil condition "no longer have any right to judge how the constitution should be administered." Kant, "On the Common Saying," 81.

20. For discussion, see Ripstein, *Force and Freedom*, 336–43.

21. There is, for Kant, a further regime category not yet mentioned: *despotism*. Under despotism, there is the rule of law, and persons have secure rights against one another. The defect in despotism is that there is insufficient separation of powers—in particular there is some fusion between the legislature and the executive. This is a problem because it risks undermining the omnilateral character of the state's exercises of power. See Kant, "On the Common Saying," 175.

is consistent with the innate right of humanity; positive legislation is only legitimate if it could be a law that free persons could impose on themselves."[22]

By contrast, when political power is exercised consistently with our right to equal freedom, this power is not only legitimate, but necessarily also defines the contours of justice. In short, the Kantian picture offers a fundamentally legal and statist view of our claims of justice. This is why there can be no legitimate injustice on the Kantian account.

This Kantian institutionalist picture of rights has the capacity to explain some widely held attitudes about justice and the exercise of state power. For example, millions of Americans believe that affirmative action policies are unfair and morally wrong. But at least some hold this view while also accepting that whether affirmative action is unjust—whether such policies violate anyone's rights—is settled by the legislature and the judiciary. Only if such policies are prohibited by law can they aptly be described as unjust. To take a different example, many Americans believe that the disparities of income and wealth between rich and poor are grossly unfair. Yet those who hold this view do not typically insist that the poor are entitled to steal money from the rich. They don't deny that this would be a violation of the rights of the rich.

These are just two examples, but it wouldn't be difficult to produce dozens more. They illustrate that many of us are inclined to distinguish between what we believe ought to be done in politics, one the one hand, and what rights and duties persons in fact possess, on the other. We distinguish between our political ideals—the ways we believe our institutions should be reformed or restructured—and the institutional reality of individual rights and duties. Suppose, for example, you are convinced that some specific theory of justice, such as Rawls's, is true. It doesn't follow that, here and now in your particular political community, you should believe that people's actual moral rights are

22. Ripstein, *Force and Freedom*, 213.

determined by Rawls's theory rather than by the laws passed and enforced by a legitimate political authority. This is in part because it might take time to realize the Rawlsian ideal. But even setting that aside, you may appreciate that not everyone agrees with you that Rawls has set out the correct theory of justice. As Gerald Gaus puts it,

> In our pluralistic world, rational and goodwilled people will not agree on an ideal moral code or theory of justice. To insist that there is a uniquely just or correct ideal code, a substantive set of rights and duties, or clear distributional norms that are authoritative for all ends up an exercise in moral authoritarianism.

Gaus elaborates,

> Free and equal persons disagree about ideal moral arrangements. A free social order is possible just because we do not have to agree on the ideal, and no ideal sets the benchmark of justice. Freedom is possible in our nonutopian world because we converge on a moral equilibrium, and truly reasonable moral persons do not condemn it as unjust simply because it falls short of their ideal, since all possible equilibria fall short of some reasonable ideals.[23]

Although Gaus's own picture of political morality departs from Kant's in various ways, in these passages he is articulating a deeply Kantian thought. We can't demand, as a matter of justice, that others comply with the ideals we believe to be true, since this would be a version of unilateralism. To achieve a social world of reciprocal or mutual freedom, the state must act as a kind of impartial arbiter. It must have the authority to determine the content of our rights and duties, even when we think the state's determinations are imperfect.

---

23. Gaus, *Order of Public Reason*, 548–49, 445.

The Indeterminacy Dilemma

Though appealing in many respects, the Kantian account faces a serious dilemma. The sole fundamental principle of justice, on the Kantian view, is the right to mutual or reciprocal freedom. But, as we have seen, this right has indeterminate prescriptions at the fine-grained level required to specify people's moral rights and duties. It doesn't entail more, or less, progressive income tax laws, it doesn't entail particular policies with regard to inheritance and bequest, it doesn't require adopting a particular view about the way legislators are selected, and so on. This substantive indeterminacy is part of the problem to which a legitimate political authority is the only solution.

But this insistence that justice is largely indeterminate across a vast array of substantive matters is difficult to reconcile with some of our considered convictions and attitudes. Look at how we typically understand and participate in substantive political debates. When we argue with one another about abortion, about tax cuts, about immigration policy, about environmental regulations, about health care, about the criminalization of recreational drugs or prostitution, or about any number of other substantive matters, we often defend our position on the grounds that it respects people's moral rights, and we often criticize the positions that we oppose as unjust, as being in violation of individual rights. For example, many of those who criticize economic inequality in the United States do not simply say this inequality is unfair, or regrettable, or that things would be better if the inequality was reduced. They also claim that the inequality constitutes an injustice.[24] Many who criticized government policies restricting social

24. Recall the claim from Bernie Sanders's website quoted in chapter 1 above: "The richest 10 percent of households have 70 percent of the wealth. The top 1% have increased their share of the wealth from 23% in 1989 to nearly 32% in 2018. The three wealthiest people in the U.S. own more wealth than the bottom 50% of Americans—160 million people. Bernie believes this is unjust and is calling for a downward transfer of wealth."

gatherings, indoor dining, and mask mandates in response to the COVID pandemic similarly argued that these policies were not merely unpleasant, or disproportionate, or inefficient. They frequently argued that these policies were a violation of individual rights, and unjust.

In short, our political disagreements are rife with justice-talk. This is not merely a matter of the words that we use when debating public policy. The concepts of justice and moral rights often explain why we are sometimes so bitterly divided over political matters. We perceive the stakes to be high because we believe that the wrong decision may involve rights violations on a massive scale.

On the Kantian view, our perceptions about the stakes of such debates involve a kind of conceptual error. Mere policy proposals—things that are not yet law—cannot be just or unjust, since they are mere ideas, and do not infringe anyone's authority to use their own means to set their own ends. If a proposal is passed by the legislature via the appropriate procedures and becomes law, then it cannot be unjust, because in virtue of having been enacted by proper procedures, it constitutes what justice requires.[25] When we vigorously debate proposed or actual laws, and criticize the proposals or laws as unjust, we are therefore guilty of a fairly serious confusion. In a legitimate state the process of legislation, enforcement, and adjudication are the means by which we conclusively resolve the indeterminacy of the fundamental innate right of reciprocal freedom. It thus makes no sense to declare potential or actual legislation (within a legitimate constitutional order) to be unjust. There is no justice without law, and the laws of a legitimate regime determine our claims of justice.

25. Kant says, about any actual law, that if it is at least possible the law is one that we could all agree to, then "it is our duty to consider the law as just, even if the people is at present in such a position or attitude of mind that it would probably refuse consent if it was consulted." He goes to provide an illustrative example involving a war and a related tax which the people oppose, but which the government imposes. Kant concludes that the tax "must be deemed rightful" since it meets the test of possible consent. Kant, "On the Common Saying," 79.

This conclusion, however, is sharply at odds with a common-sense conception of our political life. On the commonsense view, we have deep and vigorous disputes about many laws and public policies precisely because all parties to the dispute believe it is possible for laws to be unjust. We argue so fiercely about politics partly because we believe that the law ought to reflect or conform to what justice requires. On this commonsense view, there are determinate, specific pre-legislative truths about justice. When laws are inconsistent with these truths, the laws are unjust. Whatever the law might say, most people are likely to agree that it is unjust to tax the poor in order to redistribute wealth to the rich, that it is unjust to permit employers to discriminate on the basis of race or sex, that it is unjust to interfere with (non-harmful) forms of religious expression and association, and that it is unjust to criminalize most forms of political speech. These things are unjust not because the law tells us so; rather the law itself must conform to these independent truths about justice. The Kantian view is apparently unable to accommodate this commonsense view.

It's worth emphasizing that this commonsense position is compatible with accepting a great deal of indeterminacy about the requirements of justice. One can accept that justice is indeterminate about many issues—for example, about exactly what rates of income tax are required as a matter of justice, or about default rules for contract law, or whether currently incarcerated felons should have the right to vote—while insisting that, about some questions, justice is not indeterminate, and thus it's possible for ordinary laws to be unjust. It is the Kantian who is defending the more extreme and less plausible position—namely, that justice is almost completely indeterminate, and almost all ordinary legislative issues stand in need of legal resolution in order to render the requirements of justice determinate.

Whatever one thinks about our existing political practices, there's another way in which the Kantian position is counterintuitive. For the Kantian, coercion in the state of nature is always unilateral, and thus never fully rightful. No matter how sincere and well reasoned your use of coercion might be, it can never be in the service of anything more than your own interpretation of the requirements of right. The indeterminacy of justice, in conjunction with the lack of an omnilateral will, entails that no use of force in the state of nature can be fully legitimate.

This is hard to believe. Suppose we are in the state of nature and A attempts to murder B because he wants to seize the small home she has built for herself. Let's stipulate A will succeed unless he is stopped. B is fortunately able to use defensive force to repel A's aggression—she uses a stick to hit A hard enough to break a bone in his wrist, and he runs off, realizing he has miscalculated B's strength and defensive skills. Let's further stipulate that had B used any less serious form of defensive force, she would have been unable to deter A's murderous attack. My view—a view that I suspect is widely shared—is that B does nothing wrong: her use of force is fully rightful.

The Kantian, however, cannot reach this conclusion. B's use of force is unilateral—she acts on her own behalf, guided by her own judgments about the permissible use of violence. Her act thus cannot be fully rightful on the Kantian view. The Kantian can say that B is defending what she sincerely takes to be her provisional rights, and given the absence of a legitimate authority she is, in a certain sense, free to do so (though note the Kantian must say the same thing about anyone who chooses to defend A from B's act of self-defense).[26] But her use of violence is not fully rightful, because it is unilateral and she is not defending conclusive or determinate rights, given that such rights cannot exist in the absence of a legitimate political authority.

Of course, this is only one example. But we can imagine many other cases where, even in the absence of a legitimate political authority, it is intuitively clear that one person's use of defensive force is fully rightful or just. The fact that the Kantian view is

---

26. Kant, *Metaphysics of Morals*, 86.

apparently disabled from reaching this conclusion looks to be a serious defect in the account.

To avoid these implications, the Kantian might modify (or clarify) her claims about the extent to which justice is indeterminate. The Kantian could argue that justice is not indeterminate in cases such as the one described above. Although many details about our rights over our bodies and external property may be indeterminate, the Kantian could insist that it is determinately true that killing someone who poses no violent threat in order to seize resources is unjust, and thus the necessary and proportionate use of force to avert such a killing is fully rightful. (To make the point in Kantian terms, we would say that such force constitutes a hindrance to a hindrance, and as such is consistent with the right to mutual independence.) Other apparent counterexamples could then be handled in a similar fashion. For example, justice may not be fully determinate with regard to the distribution of income and wealth, but perhaps it is determinately true that income cannot be justly redistributed from the poor to the rich.

There are, however, at least two difficulties with such a response. The first is that it's very difficult to square with Kant's own writings on political philosophy, and flatly inconsistent with what many contemporary Kantians claim. The dominant view amongst contemporary Kantian political philosophers is that the substantive requirements of justice are largely indeterminate.[27] The right to independence prohibits certain forms of political domination at the extremes—for example, slavery, or the denial of property rights to some subset of citizens—but is otherwise consistent with a vast number of different potential political arrangements, provided those arrangements are conducted via the rule of law in a constitutional system with some separation of powers.

We can, however, set this worry aside given that our primary interest is philosophical, not exegetical. What really matters is not

27. See, for example, Pallikkathayil, "Deriving Morality," 137–38; Stilz, *Liberal Loyalty*, 40–41.

what Kant or contemporary Kantians say, but rather whether there's a coherent and compelling view that might be built from Kant's ideas. Thus, let's grant, for the sake of argument, that on the Kantian view justice is determinate in at least a reasonable range of cases. The Kantian now faces a different question: if justice is determinate across a non-trivial range of cases, why is the state essential to achieving just relations? The central problem with the state of nature, recall, is supposed to be that it makes freedom-as-independence impossible. It's impossible to realize mutual independence unless each person has a domain where her choices, rather than anyone else's, are sovereign. But for each person to have such a domain, each must not be subject to the unilateral judgment of others; and in the state of nature, where there are no determinate claims of justice, there can be only unilateral judgment. This is why we have to leave the state of nature—only through the rule of law can the indeterminacy of justice be resolved in a way that reflects omnilateral, rather than unilateral, judgment.

But if justice is determinate across a range of issues, it's no longer clear why there is anything objectionable about some unilateral uses of force. If, absent a state, A threatens to violate a determinate claim of B's, and B can use necessary and proportionate force to avert A's threatened injustice, why should B's use of force be problematic? Although there is a sense in which B acts unilaterally, B is not unilaterally rendering determinate something that is indeterminate. A is not being forced to serve an end or a conception of justice that he is at liberty to reject. Rather, A is simply being forced to comply with a determinate duty of justice that he owes to B, the content of which is not controlled by B's judgments or preferences. For the Kantian, this should not be construed as a problematic threat to A's independence. A is merely being hindered from interfering with B's freedom, but this kind of hindrance is fully consistent with the mutual independence of persons.

Suppose, for the sake of illustration, that we each have some determinate claims over our bodies, and justice is also at least partly determinate, in the absence of law, with regard to the acquisition of at least some rights over the external world. Now consider a state of nature where there is full compliance: that is, assume everyone complies with the determinate requirements of justice. Under these conditions, it looks possible to realize mutual independence. Each has a domain, protected by claims of justice, where their choices, rather than anyone else's, settle what can occur. It no longer looks as if we need a legitimate political authority to secure mutual independence. Mutual independence is instead secured via sufficient determinacy regarding the requirements of justice in combination with each person's willingness to act in conformity with those requirements.[28]

In sum, the Kantian faces a serious *indeterminacy dilemma.* On the one hand, she can insist that justice is largely indeterminate with regard to specific rights, duties, and institutional rules. But this flies in the face of widely shared, commonsense intuitions about what existing political debates are about, as well as generating counterintuitive claims about the use of defensive force. On the other hand, the Kantian might concede that justice is at least partly determinate across a range of substantive issues. But this concession undermines the Kantian claim that the use of force in the absence of a legitimate political authority is always problematically unilateral, and thus undermines too the argument for the constitutive role a legitimate authority plays in establishing just conditions.

Denying the Dilemma?

Let's consider some ways the Kantian might respond. She might reject the dilemma by insisting that there's a third option: a modest degree of determinacy about justice, just such as to allow us to

---

28. A Kantian might be tempted to respond that even in the absence of indeterminacy, a legitimate public authority is still required to solve the assurance problem. I address this response below.

evade both horns. On this view, justice is sufficiently determinate to enable us to evade the counterintuitive implications of the first horn, but still sufficiently indeterminate for mutual independence to be securable only through the rule of law of a legitimate political authority.

To assess this response, we require more detail concerning the degree of (in)determinacy being proposed. I can't survey all the possibilities, but the following general point will apply to all proposals. For any proposal to succeed in evading both horns of the dilemma, it must allow (a) that there are determinate, pre-institutional truths about justice with regard to some fairly specific issues (e.g., what claim rights persons have over their bodies; what forms of conduct we have claim rights against being interfered with), and yet (b) that these determinate claims are insufficient to secure for each person the minimal means required for independence in the absence of a political authority, even if we assume full compliance. I doubt that any plausible proposal can satisfy both these conditions.

The central difficulty is that Kantian independence is largely a formal, rather than a substantive, idea. Independence does not require a person to possess any particular level of material resources (beyond a minimal threshold needed to avoid being dependent on others' good will), nor does it require that a person make effective use of her physical or mental capacities. Independence only requires that there be some part of the world—a part that necessarily includes a person's body—where her choices, rather than anyone else's choices, are sovereign. So long as persons are formally equal with regard to such a sphere of freedom, mutual independence is consistent with vast differences between people's actual levels of resources, well-being, or capacity to successfully pursue their ends. As a result, a fairly minimal package of determinate rights can suffice to secure mutual independence. We don't need, for example, a determinate resolution regarding how all the world's resources should be allocated to secure mutual independence. We only need some determinacy with regard to people's claims over their bodies, and some minimal claims regarding how people can make use of the world's resources without being subject to interference from others. And these are exactly the sort of claims where it seems justice is in fact pre-institutionally determinate. The commonsense view is that we have moral rights to control our bodies, and so other people cannot make deliberate, non-consensual contact with our bodies without at least implied consent. The commonsense view is that we have broad moral rights against interference when we are expressing our views about most matters of politics, morality, or religion. The commonsense view is that it is typically wrong to interfere with someone's activities, including their use of the physical world, provided that person is not making use of things that belong to others, or threatening the rights of others. If these commonsense views about justice are correct, then even in the absence of a state, persons can be independent; each person has a pre-institutionally determinate sphere where her choices are sovereign.

It might seem that the preceding line of thought ignores a crucial fact: in the absence of a state there is no agent to provide genuine assurance that persons' rights will be respected. In a state of nature, the security of our rights depends on others' willingness to comply with their duties. Doesn't this fatally undermine the sense in which persons can be independent in the state of nature, since the security of our rights is contingent on the good will of others? The Kantian can thus insist that even if we grant the determinacy of justice across a non-trivial range of issues, reciprocal freedom is still only possible within a legitimate political order.

But I think this Kantian response does not succeed.[29] The response alleges that the security of our rights is contingent on the will or dispositions of others in the state of nature in a way that it is not in a legitimate political order. But, as a descriptive matter, this claim seems false. The state and its institutions are not

29. For a similar objection to the Kantian position, see Kolodny, "Being Under the Power." For an insightful response on the Kantian's behalf, see Sinclair, "Power of Public Positions."

independent machines—they depend for their success on the attitudes and dispositions of a great many people. We know from experience that political institutions can function well or badly depending on people's attitudes and beliefs. In extreme cases, states can fail when enough people are unwilling to support its institutions and policies. On the flip-side, we can imagine small pre-legal societies where members, for the most part, willingly respect the rights of others despite the absence of a central enforcement mechanism. So I do not think the Kantian can be understood as making a descriptive or non-normative claim about the relative security of rights.

Alternatively, we might understand the Kantian to be making a normative or conceptual claim. Whereas it is constitutive of a legitimate political order that people's moral rights are upheld—this is the defining function of a legitimate order—this is not a constitutive fact about the state of nature. Whether people's rights are upheld in the state of nature is contingent on the good will of others. And that is why we lack independence in the state of nature, but not in a legitimate political order.

This version of the Kantian response also does not succeed, however. Just as the Kantian stipulates that it is constitutive of a legitimate political order that it upholds people's moral rights, we can stipulate that it is constitutive of just relations in the state of nature that each person is robustly committed to fulfilling her duties of justice. The Kantian cannot object to this claim by pointing out that, as a matter of empirical fact, whether just relations obtain is contingent on people's dispositions, since this is also true of a political order, and the Kantian position currently under consideration is supposed to be a normative or conceptual one.

In sum, I am skeptical that there is a modest degree of determinacy about justice that would allow the Kantian successfully to evade both horns of the indeterminacy dilemma. If the Kantian concedes that justice is sufficiently determinate for the first horn of the dilemma to be evaded—by concluding that we have determinate rights over our bodies and also with regard to a range of our non-harmful behavior—it's difficult to avoid the conclusion that the use of force outside a political order can be consistent with mutual independence, and that a political order may be inessential to realizing mutual independence.

Conclusion

Many find the Kantian picture of political philosophy compelling. It is centered around a conception of independence that nicely captures the relational nature of freedom as a political value. Rather than being presented as a contingently necessary evil, political institutions are instead presented as constitutive of realizing this relationship, and thus the only way to live together on just terms. The Kantian picture also explains why legitimate states can vary widely in terms of their laws and policies. This variation is unsurprising if the requirements of justice are largely indeterminate, requiring institutional specification for their realization.

This last feature of the Kantian view promises to dissolve the puzzle of legitimate injustice. As we saw in chapter 2, proponents of Justice First tell us that if (as we should) we accept justice as the first virtue of social institutions, we must give up the third claim that forms the puzzle: we must accept that much of what state officials do in liberal democratic societies is illegitimate. On the Kantian picture, we are not forced to make this choice. Because the right to external freedom is largely indeterminate, the ordinary laws within a legitimate democratic community cannot be unjust. Our legal institutions are instead essential to rendering the requirements of justice determinate. We can thus maintain that justice is the first virtue of social institutions while also insisting that state officials act legitimately in enforcing most ordinary legislation.

I have argued, however, that this solution to the puzzle exposes the Kantian view to a serious dilemma. If the Kantian insists that justice is largely indeterminate in the absence of legal institutions, this flies in the face of commonsense views about our political disagreements as well as commonsense judgments concerning rights to defend oneself from wrongful aggressors. To evade this first horn, the Kantian can concede that justice is not so indeterminate, but this concession threatens to undermine the core Kantian ideas that force cannot be rightful in the absence of a political order, and that independence can only be secured through legitimate political institutions.

The shared assumption of the Kantian view and Justice First is that state officials do not act legitimately if the particular laws that they enforce are unjust. In the next chapter we will consider an approach that rejects this assumption: one that emphasizes the instrumental value of relations of authority, and thereby promises to explain, rather than deny, the phenomenon of legitimate injustice.

4

The Instrumental Value
of Institutions

WHAT, IF ANYTHING, could justify the existence of institutions wielding political authority? What, if anything, could justify imbuing officials with so much power over so many people? Perhaps the most obvious answer to this question is that such institutions are justified insofar as they deliver benefits to us that we can't more effectively realize in some other way. There's a plausible case to be made that the institutions of government (or at least some types of government) are, in fact, of enormous instrumental value to us. Governments can, among other things, help us solve coordination problems and collective action problems, they can provide ways of pooling risks across persons and generations, they can provide security, they can create currencies, and they can enact and enforce rules to regulate conduct in ways that can benefit all of us. These are just some of the ways in which governing institutions are instrumentally valuable.

Almost all of these good things that governments can do for us depend, however, on political institutions having some form of authority. To solve coordination and collective action problems, to provide security, to do all the good things listed in the preceding paragraph, governments must at least possess de facto authority. A government has de facto authority when it is, for the most part, able to get people to do the things that it directs them to do.[1] In theory, this authority could be achieved purely through coercion: people do what the government commands not out of any sense of obligation, but only because they fear the sanctions those in power can impose. But wielding power in this way is notoriously unstable and inefficient. Without any sense amongst the population that the government ought in fact to be obeyed, it is burdensome for governments to do the monitoring and coercion required to ensure widespread compliance, and the instrumental benefits of governing institutions may be compromised or lost. Political institutions are much more likely to be of instrumental value when people take themselves to be under at least a prima facie duty to comply with the directives the government issues.

If a government does in fact have the authority to issue directives in a way that generates a duty to comply, and if enough people accept this fact, then the government can provide us with many important benefits. For this reason, relations of authority can be instrumentally valuable. Having someone in charge with the authority to boss us around can help us do things together that we would struggle, or fail, to do without that relation of authority. This offers a compelling way to understand how, and under what conditions, political institutions can be legitimate: political institutions have actual authority over us when this relationship of authority would be sufficiently beneficial for us.

This picture of political legitimacy has several advantages, among which it offers a potential solution to the puzzle of legitimate injustice. There can be sufficient instrumental justifications for institutions even when they make mistakes. Fire departments, for example, are not perfect, but they still deliver considerable

1. Although this is a widely accepted definition of de facto authority, some philosophers prefer a narrower definition that additionally requires certain attitudes on the part of most alleged subjects.

instrumental benefits that likely outweigh the costs of the occasional errors firefighters make. Suppose the same is true about relations of political authority. Suppose, that is, that even though our political institutions sometimes err, this doesn't suffice to undermine the instrumental justification for having political institutions with authority. This idea might allow us to affirm all three claims that constitute the puzzle of legitimate injustice. If the best means to securing justice is an authority-wielding government that nevertheless sometimes makes mistakes, then its errors do not undermine the justification for its authority. The best way to respect the priority of justice may be to have a political institution with broad practical authority, broad enough to include mistakes about justice.

This chapter explores these ideas in greater detail, with a particular focus on Joseph Raz's influential service conception of authority. The chapter begins with a discussion of the nature of practical authority, distinguishing it from other, related, notions. We then turn to consider political authority, and what reasons there might be to consider certain political institutions to have genuine practical authority. We'll look at how this picture of authority offers an apparent solution to the puzzle of legitimate injustice. I then introduce some preliminary worries about the instrumental account of political authority, though I suggest Raz's account of authority has, subject to modifications, the resources to meet these challenges. Nevertheless, I maintain that, despite appearances, the instrumental account of political authority cannot successfully explain the phenomenon of legitimate injustice. The problem, in brief, is that the general instrumental value of an institution cannot justify the performance of particular acts or policies when those acts or policies don't deliver the instrumental benefits. I consider some potential replies to this objection, but I argue that these replies do not succeed. The chapter concludes, in part, by considering the more general implications for any instrumental conception of political authority.

Practical Authority

What does it mean for one person to be an authority with regard to another? One sense of authority is *epistemic*. My doctor is an epistemic authority for me about my health. My mechanic is an epistemic authority for me about the maintenance of my car. A distinguished professor specializing in sixteenth-century European history is an epistemic authority for me about that era. An epistemic authority knows more than others do about some topic, and as a result those others have good reasons to believe what that authority tells them within the authority's area of expertise.

Because epistemic authorities know more than others, it also often makes sense to follow their directions. When my doctor tells me I should cut down on salt in my diet, I have a compelling reason to reduce the amount of salt I consume. When my mechanic tells me I need to get new brake pads for the car, I probably should do that. When the distinguished professor of history tells me I should remove a misleading claim about the sixteenth century in a footnote of an academic paper, it seems like that's what I ought to do. It's thus tempting to assimilate epistemic authority to *practical* authority—to conclude that what makes someone a practical authority is the fact that they know more than you about a particular domain.

But this assimilation would be a mistake.[2] Epistemic authorities need not be practical authorities, and practical authorities need not be epistemic authorities. My doctor knows more than I do about the positive health benefits of reducing the amount of salt in my diet. But it doesn't follow that she has practical authority over me about this decision—I'm not under a duty or an obligation to take this step simply because she tells me to. The same is true about my mechanic and the distinguished history professor.

2. See, for example, David Estlund's discussion of the expert/boss fallacy in Estlund, *Democratic Authority*, ch. 3.

What they tell me is best construed as advice. I have good reasons to follow their advice, but I'm at liberty to make my own decision. I can weigh the epistemic value of their advice against my own assessment of the situation when deciding what I'm going to do.

Practical authority clearly involves something more. Consider a paradigm case of a practical authority: a commanding officer in the army giving a lawful order to a subordinate. The commanding officer is not giving the subordinate advice about what to do. He is giving the subordinate a command. The subordinate is not (within limits) at liberty to weigh up the value of obeying this command against his own assessment of the situation. Instead, the command appears to exclude, or preempt, the subordinate's own reasoning about the situation. It doesn't matter if the subordinate thinks there is a better way to do things. The command takes precedence and typically settles what the subordinate must do.

This preemptory feature of commands seems to be at the heart of what it is for one agent to be a practical authority with regard to another. When a practical authority issues a directive, this directive seems to provide an *exclusionary reason* for the subject of the authority.[3] An exclusionary reason is a second-order reason that requires the subject to exclude some first-order reasons from deliberation when deciding how to act. The subordinate's first-order reasons might include self-interested reasons, facts about what would be best for the platoon, and so on. The commanding officer's order serves to exclude all those reasons from the subordinate's deliberations, and replace them with a reason to do as the officer has commanded. Joseph Raz describes this as the

> *Preemption Thesis*: the fact that an authority requires performance of an action is a reason for its performance which is not to be added to all other relevant reasons when assessing what to do, but should exclude and take the place of some of them.[4]

---

3. For an early discussion of exclusionary reasons, see Raz, *Authority of Law*, 17–18.
4. Raz, *Morality of Freedom*, 46.

The idea that some of our first-order reasons can be excluded or preempted in this way is not unique to the context of authority. Promises are also standardly understood to work in this way. If I promise to give you a ride to the airport tomorrow, my promissory obligation to you is not something that I weigh against all the reasons I have for and against taking you to the airport tomorrow. It rather serves to exclude some reasons that might otherwise bear on my decision (e.g., that I find myself in the middle of reading a novel that I don't want to put down).

If this capacity to preempt or exclude first-order reasons is a defining feature of practical authority, it's easy to see why there's no necessary connection between epistemic authority and practical authority. When my mechanic tells me what he thinks I should do about my brakes, he isn't purporting to preempt or exclude my own deliberations about my car. He's simply giving me his expert opinion about my car. Our mechanic-customer relationship doesn't require him to have practical authority over me in the way that the commanding officer does with regard to his subordinate. Indeed, one needn't be an epistemic authority to be a practical authority. The commanding officer might not know more about military tactics, or what best motivates his platoon, as compared to the subordinate. But he can still have practical authority, by virtue of his rank.

What makes one person a practical authority over another? Consent is perhaps the most obvious basis for practical authority. If A consents to B's practical authority with regard to some domain, then (at least within limits) B becomes a practical authority over A with regard to that domain. People should have the freedom to enter into various relations of authority if they wish. Consent can thus explain a range of cases of practical authority: for example, the practical authority that employers sometimes have over their employees.

Other apparent instances of practical authority cannot be explained via consent, however. The existence of parental authority suggests that certain relationships might make one person a practical authority over another even in the absence of consent. But there are other apparent examples that involve neither consent nor any sort of relationship. Consider:

The Accident: A serious car crash has just occurred at an intersection, and several people have been badly injured. The paramedics have been called, but it will be some time before they arrive and the injured people need urgent care. Fortunately, there are four bystanders at the scene, and one of them happens to be doctor. The doctor begins issuing orders to the other three bystanders, telling one to apply pressure to a wound, telling another to fetch equipment from the doctor's car, and telling the third to hold an injured person's head steady.

The doctor seems to have practical authority over the other bystanders in this case. The doctor isn't giving the bystanders mere advice—he's issuing something more like commands. The other bystanders shouldn't weigh the doctor's directives against their own assessments of the first-order reasons: they should take his directives as excluding and taking the place of those reasons. Why? It cannot be the mere fact that the doctor is an epistemic authority on medical matters, since we've seen that epistemic authority doesn't necessarily translate into practical authority. Why are things different in this case?

Raz offers a compelling and influential answer. According to Raz, the doctor in our case has authority over the other bystanders because the bystanders can better comply with the reasons for action that apply to them if he has this authority. Here is how he formulates the idea:

The Normal Justification Thesis: the normal way to establish that a person has authority over another person involves showing that the alleged subject is likely better to comply with reasons which apply to him (other than the alleged authoritative directives) if he accepts the directives of the alleged authority as authoritatively binding and tries to follow them, rather than by trying to follow the reasons which apply to him directly.[5]

We can assume that each of the bystanders has a weighty reason to provide aid to those who are injured. This reason will be limited by other considerations; for example, we cannot expect the bystanders to make supererogatory sacrifices. But within those limits, they have a reason, indeed likely a duty, to help the victims of the accident until the paramedics arrive. But since the other three bystanders lack any medical expertise, they might not do a very good job helping the victims if they try and work things out for themselves. The best way for the bystanders to comply with their reason or duty to aid the victims is by taking the doctor's directives as authoritatively binding. That's how they can best do what they have reason to do. The normal justification thesis can thus explain how relations of authority arise in the absence of consent, and in the absence of some prior relationship. It thus looks like a promising way to explain how relations of political authority might arise.

Before turning to the political realm, it's worth noting a few features about this picture of practical authority. First, the authority relation is justified in instrumental terms. The relation of authority is justified when, and because, it will enable those subject to the authority to better comply with their own reasons for action. Because the authority relation is conceptualized as helping those subject to the authority better conform to their own reasons for action, Raz's account is aptly known as the *service conception* of authority.

Second, the authority relation can be limited in scope in various ways. One person can be an authority over others about a particular topic or task, but not with regard to anything else. This is what happens in the accident scenario. The doctor has authority over the other bystanders with regard to the urgent project of aiding the victims, but not anything else. He cannot, for example, order

5. Raz, *Morality of Freedom*, 53.

one of the bystanders to fetch his dry cleaning or wash his car. Who is subject to the authority is also limited in scope. If an ER surgeon happens upon the scene of the accident after the doctor has already started issuing directives to the other bystanders, the surgeon likely won't be subject to the doctor's authority, because it won't be true that the surgeon can best comply with her reasons for action by taking orders from the doctor.

Third, the reasons for which a practical authority helps its subjects better comply must be reasons that already exist independent of the authority's directives. Raz refers to this as the *dependence thesis*.[6] We see this clearly in the example of the accident. The bystanders have reasons, independent of the doctor's directives, to provide aid to the victims. Obeying the doctor's directives is simply a better way for the bystanders to try and comply with those reasons. But reasons that subjects acquire only by virtue of the commands of an authority cannot themselves legitimize those commands. For example, once a commanding officer orders his subordinate to do something, the subordinate acquires a new reason to obey: namely, he will be sanctioned if he doesn't. But that reason cannot contribute to the question of whether the commanding officer satisfies the normal justification thesis.

Finally, the duty to obey need not be understood as absolute or taking lexical priority over all other concerns. The orders of a legitimate authority will typically preempt or exclude some, but not all, of the subject's first-order reasons.[7] The doctor's directives, for instance, exclude and take the place of the other bystanders' deliberations about how best to aid the victims of the accident, but they don't exclude reasons in relation to other matters. If one of the bystanders knows that being late for his meeting will cause

---

6. Raz, *Morality of Freedom*, 47.

7. In the Razian picture, "legitimate authority" refers to a political authority that satisfies the normal justification thesis with regard to at least some subjects at least some of the time. See Raz, *Morality of Freedom*, 53.

him to lose his job, he can weigh this reason against any directives issued by the doctor.

In sum, legitimate or genuine practical authorities issue commands that function to exclude and take the place of some of the subject's first-order reasons for action. Some authorities are made legitimate via the consent of those subject to the authority. But even in the absence of consent, it is often argued, relations of authority can be instrumentally justified. In particular, when the relation of authority serves those subject to the authority by helping them better comply with their own reasons for action, the authority can be legitimate for those subjects.

Political Authority

With this instrumental picture of authority to hand, we can turn to consider whether the authority of political institutions can plausibly be justified in this way.

There are some reasons to be skeptical. Examples like that above of the accident have several distinctive features. A small group of people all have the same weighty reason to engage in a project, and there is an agent with special expertise regarding how the project can best be carried out. Modern political societies don't look much like this. There are millions of people who all have very different plans and projects, and thus very different reasons for action. There are also no widely acknowledged experts concerning central political questions. We are sharply divided concerning the answers to these questions and thus we will have widely differing views on who the relevant political experts might be, if indeed there are any.

Despite these substantial disanalogies, there are good reasons to suspect that political institutions might, under certain conditions, satisfy something like Raz's normal justification thesis. Consider the duties of justice that we owe to one another.

First, suppose that we owe each other duties of rescue or mutual aid. We ought to make efforts to save others from dire circumstances when we can do so at reasonable cost. Further suppose that, for familiar reasons, life in the absence of political institutions—in the state of nature—would be dire for many people. It would be dangerous, unpredictable, and mutually beneficial forms of cooperation would be very limited. We have a duty to rescue each other from this condition if we can do so at reasonable cost. Creating and sustaining minimally decent political institutions looks like a way of fulfilling this duty.[8] Political institutions can provide order and security, they can create laws and thereby stabilize people's expectations, and they can create and enforce property rights that make possible a vast array of mutually beneficial transactions and relationships. But, in order to deliver these benefits at a reasonable cost, political institutions need people reliably to comply with their directives. There is thus a straightforward instrumental argument as to how minimally decent political institutions might satisfy the normal justification thesis. We all have compelling reasons to rescue each other from the dire conditions of the state of nature. We can best comply with these reasons by taking the state's directives as authoritatively binding and following them, rather than by trying to directly comply with the reasons ourselves. We don't need to assume that governments or officials have anything like the kind of expertise that the doctor does in our earlier example. It's rather that governments can solve collective action problems on a scale that isn't possible without authoritative institutions.

The preceding argument does depend, however, on at least one contentious premise: namely, that life for many people in the state of nature would be dire—something from which they have a claim to be rescued. So let's drop this assumption and replace it with something less grim. Suppose that life in the absence of political institutions wouldn't be too bad, because people are, by and large, disposed to avoid violent conflicts whenever possible, and to

8. For versions of this argument from natural duty, see Wellman, "Liberalism, Samaritanism"; Wellman and Simmons, *Is There a Duty*, ch. 1.

cooperate with each other for mutual gain. Even with these more optimistic assumptions in place, the state of nature suffers from a fundamental defect, one that played a large role in the Kantian picture of political morality considered in chapter 3: the indeterminacy of justice at the level of specific rights over bodies and property. This indeterminacy makes it difficult for us to realize many gains from cooperation. Without widely accepted and authoritative mechanisms to determine property rights, we lose the opportunities for mutually beneficial commerce, and for many other activities that require stable expectations about rights. Even were the predicament of most not dire, we would each still have strong reasons to resolve the indeterminacy of individual rights. We would all greatly benefit from having a political and legal regime that could render determinate our specific rights via legislative, executive, and judicial branches. So even if we make less pessimistic assumptions about the state of nature, it still looks like there might be a compelling instrumental argument for the existence of political authority.

The preceding argument, however, is still very general. It starts from a claim about the indeterminacy of rights, and ends with a fairly general conclusion about the instrumental value of political authority. So let's consider a third view. Suppose that there is less indeterminacy about moral rights than the preceding argument assumes. Does this undercut the instrumental argument for political authority? Not necessarily. To begin, even if there is less indeterminacy about rights than this argument assumes, there is still surely some such indeterminacy. And this remaining degree of indeterminacy will still prove problematic. It will thwart our ability to pursue securely certain projects and forms of cooperation. So we will still have instrumental reasons to have relations of political authority, to resolve the remaining indeterminacy; it's just that the scope of that authority will be more restricted.

There may also be coordination and collective action problems that aren't generated by indeterminacy of moral rights, but could most effectively be solved by having effective political institutions.

Take carbon emissions as an example. The main problem here may have nothing to do with people's moral rights being indeterminate. It may instead be something more like a prisoner's dilemma. We each often have compelling reasons to engage in activities that produce emissions. We also know that the emissions that we each individually produce via these activities make virtually no difference to the global total. If most other people decrease their emitting activities, we can thus continue with our emitting activities without doing any real harm. And if most other people are not going to reduce their emissions, then there's no real point in reducing our own since this won't make a difference. In other words, regardless of what others do, the rational strategy is to refuse to reduce personal emission levels. But if everyone follows this strategy, it can have collectively disastrous consequences. One way to dissolve prisoner's dilemmas is to have a practical authority dictate what each must do. If the directives of the authority exclude and take the place of each person's first-order reasoning about what would be best, we can avoid the collectively disastrous outcome. Practical authorities can also sometimes be the most effective way to solve coordination problems— for example, which side of the road to drive on, or which standards to adopt for regulating various products.

This is a more piecemeal argument for the instrumental value of political authority. It doesn't move from sweeping claims about the dire situation in the state of nature or the indeterminacy of moral rights to a general conclusion about the instrumental value of political authority. Instead, it points out that there may be particular problems that are most effectively resolved via institutions with practical authority over specific domains. The piecemeal approach thus vindicates not a general duty to obey the directives of a political authority, but only a duty to obey some of the directives. But perhaps that's all we should want from an account of political authority. Maybe the commonsense view that there's a general duty to obey the law is mistaken.[9] Why suppose political

9. See, for example, Raz, *Authority of Law*, 227–43.

institutions have authority unless the exercise of the alleged authority is in fact instrumentally beneficial?

I've sketched three different arguments for the instrumental value of (at least some) political authority: an argument that supposes circumstances for many would be dire absent such an authority; an argument from the indeterminacy of principles of right; and an argument based on the intractability of particular collective action problems. These aren't the only ways to argue for the instrumental value of political institutions, and for our purposes we don't need to decide which argument might be best. It's enough to observe that, if something like Raz's normal justification thesis is true, then there are likely good instrumental arguments for at least some forms of political authority. There are simply so many potential ways relations of authority, suitably designed, might provide us with substantial benefits that couldn't more effectively be achieved in some other way.

The instrumental account of political authority has some attractive features. First, it offers an intuitively compelling picture of what we typically think political institutions are supposed to do: they are supposed to serve the governed, to work for our benefit by, for example, helping us to solve large-scale problems of coordination or cooperation that might be difficult to solve in the absence of such institutions.

Second, the account explains what many take to be central or defining features of political institutions: the authority to command and the duty to obey the law. If the instrumental argument for political authority is sound, this apparently oppressive or restrictive relationship is in fact essential in helping us do what we have independent reasons to do.

Finally, the account seems likely to have the right scope. It won't grant legitimacy to political institutions too readily without making the bar for legitimacy too high. Regimes that fail to solve some of the main problems of collective life—for example, regimes that don't provide stability and assurance concerning the rule of law, or regimes that aim primarily to benefit only a ruling elite—will almost certainly not satisfy the normal justification thesis. But regimes don't have to be perfectly just—indeed they might commit or fail to prevent a great deal of injustice—in order to be instrumentally justified. This coheres with the widely shared view that regimes don't have to be fully just to be legitimate. The next section considers this feature of the view in more detail.

Instrumentally Justified Mistakes

Let's suppose that the normal justification thesis, or something close to it, is true. In particular, let's consider the position of a low-level state official, O. Given his role, O has reasons to serve members of the public, to provide them with certain benefits that follow from his role and the more general institution to which he belongs. O might be a police officer, or a tax official, or an official who works in the department of public housing. Assume that the best way for O to act in accordance with the reasons connected to his job—the best way for him to serve members of the public—is not by deliberating about all the first-order considerations in each case, but rather by accepting the directives of his superiors as authoritatively binding: by understanding those directives as excluding and taking the place of the first-order reasons. In other words, let's assume the normal justification thesis applies to the relation between O and his superiors.

Of course, O's superiors (and ultimately the legislature that they serve) aren't infallible; they are going to make mistakes. But this needn't undercut their authority with regard to O. Even if O's superiors sometimes err and direct O to do things that aren't for the best, it can still be true that, in general, that O will better serve members of the public by following as authoritative the directives of his superiors than by trying to reason everything through himself.

What happens, then, when O's superiors issue a mistaken directive to O? In particular, what happens when O's superiors mistakenly direct him to do something that is unjust? The answer, according to the instrumental account, would seem to be that O is in fact justified in obeying the directive.[10] After all, the best way for O to serve those over whom he exercises power is to obey the directives of his superiors—to treat those directives as excluding and replacing the first-order reasons he would otherwise weigh up to figure out what to do. O would thus be doing something unjustified if he considered each directive on its merits and decided for himself whether or not to comply with it. So, although in this instance O's superiors have erred and directed him to commit an injustice, O has a justification for obeying the mistaken directive.[11]

If O is justified in obeying the directive, then we are half-way toward explaining the phenomenon of legitimate injustice. Recall the account of legitimacy with which we have been working throughout the book: laws are legitimate when state officials act permissibly in enforcing these laws, and they have rights against harmful interference with their enforcement. If O has a justification for obeying, then O acts permissibly in obeying.

But what about the second half of legitimacy? Does O have rights against harmful interference when he commits the injustice? At first glance, this might seem difficult to understand. O is committing an injustice and thereby threatening someone's, or some group of people's, moral rights. When we threaten the moral rights of others, we typically render ourselves liable to defensive harm; that is, we forfeit rights against the imposition of necessary and proportionate harm that might serve to avert our unjust

10. For an argument to this effect see Parry, "Authority and Harm." Raz is also clear that mistaken directives from an authority that satisfy the normal justification thesis are binding. See Raz, *Morality of Freedom*, 47–48.

11. This conclusion is noteworthy, since many have assumed that there are, at most, three possible justifications for acting in ways that would ordinarily constitute the violation of another person's moral rights: (1) a liability justification, (2) a lesser-evil justification, and (3) an agent-relative prerogative. The instrumental argument for authority thus apparently provides a less well-recognized fourth justification. Parry makes this point in "Authority and Harm."

threat. If, for example, Albert culpably tries to murder Betty because she has rejected his romantic overtures, Albert becomes liable to necessary and proportionate defensive harm, which is to say that he lacks claim rights against the imposition of this harm. But things are different for our state official O. Unlike Albert, O has a justification for what he's doing. And there are good reasons to believe that if someone has a justification for Φ-ing, that person cannot be liable for Φ-ing.[12] To begin, there is intuitive support for this conclusion. Consider a police officer confronting a hostage-taker. The hostage-taker has decided to prove his seriousness by killing ten of the hostages. The only way for the officer to save the ten from being killed is to detonate an explosive device that will kill the hostage-taker, but doing so will also foreseeably kill an innocent bystander. If these facts provide the police officer with a lesser-evil justification for detonating the explosive device, it seems counterintuitive to insist that the police officer also becomes liable to defensive harm—that he forfeits his rights against harm if harming him could somehow save the innocent bystander. And there is a deeper explanation for this intuition: the police officer does not act wrongly in detonating the device. He has sufficiently compelling reasons to perform the act, reasons weighty enough to outweigh or override the rights of the innocent bystander. When someone responds correctly to the reasons that apply to their situation, they shouldn't forfeit their moral rights. They are categorically different than a culpable would-be murderer.

If the preceding argument is sound—if justification defeats liability—then our state official O is not only justified in obeying the mistaken directive of his superiors; he also retains rights against defensive harm when carrying out this directive. We have thus arrived at an apparent explanation of legitimate injustice. Sometimes the best way for state officials to serve those over whom they exercise power is to follow orders—to treat the

---

12. The most influential proponent of this conclusion is Jeff McMahan. See, for example, McMahan, *Killing in War*, 42–45.

directives of their superiors as excluding and replacing the first-order reasons about which they would otherwise deliberate. This can be true even though the superiors are not infallible and will sometimes err and issue mistaken, even unjust, directives. Although the state official commits injustice by following the directive, he has a sound justification for doing so, one that is rooted in a commitment to best serving the members of the public.

This explanation, moreover, apparently allows us to affirm all three claims that constitute the puzzle of legitimate injustice:

1) "Justice is the first virtue of social institutions, as truth is of systems of thought. A theory however elegant and economical must be rejected or revised if it is untrue; likewise laws and institutions no matter how efficient and well-arranged must be reformed or abolished if they are unjust."[13]

2) Some ordinary laws in liberal democratic societies are unjust.

3) Many of these laws can be legitimate: that is, state officials act permissibly in enforcing these laws and they have rights against harmful interference while enforcing them.

We have just seen how proponents of the instrumental argument for political authority can affirm the third claim. When the normal justification thesis is satisfied, state officials have a justification for following the directives of their superiors, and if justification defeats liability, they will retain claim rights against interference even when the directives they enforce are mistakes. This explanation also allows us to accept the second claim. Relations of authority can obtain even when the authority in question makes mistakes, including mistakes about justice. Most notably, the explanation also seems consistent with endorsing the first claim. We can accept that justice is the first virtue of social institutions, but acknowledge that sometimes the best feasible way to pursue justice is by having relations of authority—by having state

13. Rawls, *Theory of Justice*, 3.

officials follows orders even though their superiors are not infallible. If the alternative of having state officials try and reason things through themselves in each instance would produce greater injustice, then the instrumental argument for authority under consideration is consistent with the spirit of the first claim.[14]

A further virtue of this picture—as of the more general account of authority on which it rests—is that it seems that the account of legitimate injustice is neither over- nor under-inclusive. Because an alleged authority must meet the normal justification thesis to be legitimate, regimes that are clearly suboptimal in terms of their competence or their aims relative to feasible alternatives won't have legitimate authority. At the same time, regimes don't have to meet impossibly high standards to satisfy the normal justification thesis. Even regimes that make a lot of mistakes might still be ones that satisfy the normal justification thesis for their officials on a wide range of issues.

In sum, the instrumental argument for authority appears to provide a compelling solution to the puzzle of legitimate injustice. I will argue, however, that appearances are here deceptive. The instrumental account cannot, in fact, deliver all these benefits. But before proceeding to that argument, it's worth pausing to consider some other worries that might be expressed with regard to the instrumental picture of political authority.

Preliminary Worries

In this section I present some objections to the instrumental argument for authority. I do not believe any of these objections are fatal to the argument, though some of them illustrate the need to limit its scope. As a reminder, here is Raz's

14. It's worth recalling that, after having called justice the first virtue of social institutions, Rawls goes on to clarify that "[t]he only thing that permits us to acquiesce in an erroneous theory is the lack of a better one; analogously, an injustice is tolerable only when it is necessary to avoid an even greater injustice." Rawls, *Theory of Justice*, 4.

Normal Justification Thesis: the normal way to establish that a person has authority over another person involves showing that the alleged subject is likely better to comply with reasons which apply to him (other than the alleged authoritative directives) if he accepts the directives of the alleged authority as authoritatively binding and tries to follow them, rather than by trying to follow the reasons which apply to him directly.[15]

An initial worry about this thesis is that it is too broad in scope.[16] It focuses on the reasons that apply to a subject, and Raz is clear that this includes the entirety of the subject's reasons for action. But it's not difficult to imagine counterexamples when the scope of the thesis is interpreted so broadly. Suppose you are at risk of being late to watch a film that you are keen to see, but you're in an unfamiliar city and uncertain how to get to the movie theater most quickly. A friend who knows the city well gives you directions. The normal justification thesis is met: you will best comply with the reasons that apply to you by taking her directions as authoritatively binding, rather than by trying to figure things out for yourself. But surely it does not follow that your friend is in fact a legitimate authority over you in this matter, or that you have duty to follow her directions? You might be unwise or foolish, but you wouldn't be acting in the wrong, in failing to accept her as an authority. There are many other cases where someone is an epistemic authority on some topic (your doctor or history professor, for example), and because they are an epistemic authority it would be best for you to follow their guidance or advice, and yet it does not seem correct to say that that they are a practical authority—that they can issue binding directives that you are duty-bound to obey.

In these sorts of cases, whether or not the subject complies with the reasons that apply to her doesn't seem to be anyone else's business. No one else typically has the standing to demand that you

15. Raz, *Morality of Freedom*, 53.

16. Here I summarize an objection first presented in Quong, *Liberalism without Perfection*, 113–20.

get to your movie on time, or take the best possible care of your health, or avoid embarrassing errors when publishing your scholarly work. And so even though you have good reasons to realize these aims, the reasons don't seem to be the right sort to generate relations of authority.[17]

We can fix this problem, however, by adjusting the scope of the normal justification thesis. Instead of including all the subject's reasons, we could limit the thesis to reasons of duty or obligation to others.[18] We would thereby limit relations of authority to cases where the subject can best comply with her duties or obligations to others by accepting the alleged authority's directives as binding. This allows us to make sense of the difference between the case of the accident (where the doctor, intuitively, is an authority in relation to the other bystanders), as opposed to cases like the friend offering directions to the movie theater, where intuitively there is no relation of authority. From this point forward, I'll assume we are working with this narrower conception of the normal justification thesis.

You might worry that the instrumental view of authority is too inclusive in yet another way. Raz's normal justification thesis is comparative: the question is whether you can better comply with the reasons that apply to you by taking some alleged authority's directives as binding as compared, say, to reasoning things through for yourself, or to following some other feasible strategy. This makes the bar for genuine authority contingent on various facts about alternative strategies—for example, how well the subject can work things out for herself, or the availability of other feasible

17. A defender of the normal justification thesis may point out that we also often have compelling reasons of autonomy—to make important choices for ourselves—and once these reasons are taken into account the alleged counterexamples to the normal justification thesis are not in fact counterexamples. But although the appeal to autonomy may limit the range of counterexamples, it does not eliminate all of them. There is, for example, no important reason to make your own autonomous decision about how to get to the movie theater on time.

18. I make this proposal in Quong, *Liberalism without Perfection*, 128.

mechanisms of compliance with her reasons. This might make the account of authority seem contingent in the wrong way. Putative authority A might be very corrupt, negligent, or have malicious aims, but so long as the alternative strategies available to subject S would have even worse results than obeying A's directives, A's authority over S is genuine.

If we focus on the normal justification thesis with the narrower scope—restricted to best complying with duties and obligations to others—I believe this worry becomes less stark. Return to our example of the accident. Suppose the doctor is a bit drunk and thus more likely to make errors. What matters still, surely, is the comparative judgment: will the other bystanders better comply with their duties to aid the victims by following the doctor's orders than by trying to figure things out for themselves? If the bystanders have a better chance of aiding the victims by following the doctor's orders even when he's drunk, then they owe it to the victims to do so. Similarly, if citizens of a country can best fulfil the duties of justice that they owe to one another by taking government officials' directives as authoritatively binding, then they owe it to one another to do so, and this can be true even if the government is in various ways corrupt, negligent, or malicious.

Finally, some might press the following objection. Political regimes in the real world claim a very general kind of authority over their citizens: they issue laws that regulate almost all aspects of people's lives. Governments claim, among other things, the authority to regulate the substances that we ingest, the way we can build our homes, the type of animals we can keep as pets, the type of commercial contracts we may and may not enter into, the number of hours we can work, and so on. But, says the skeptic, it's surely implausible to suppose that existing governments in fact satisfy the normal justification thesis for everyone in their territory over this vast array of issues. It's not possible that, for each of us, the best way we can comply with our duties and obligations to others is to treat our government as having this kind of extraordinary authority over almost all aspects of our lives. Put differently, the instrumental argument for authority seems unable to vindicate the general duty to obey the law that many take to be constitutive of political life.

Rather than viewing this as a serious objection, proponents of the instrumental argument tend to embrace it as a feature. There is, according to Raz, likely no general kind of political authority. Instead,

[t]hose who do not voluntarily or semi-voluntarily place themselves under the authority of relatively just governments are under a partial and qualified obligation to recognize the authority of such a government in their country. In particular its authority should be recognized to the extent necessary to enable it to secure goals, which individuals have reason to secure, for which social co-ordination is necessary or helpful, and where this is the most promising way of achieving them. Considerations of this kind would lead to a good deal of common authority, that is they would legitimate the authority of a government over all its subjects regarding a certain range of issues. Beyond that it will have authority regarding other issues which is based on other considerations, such as superior expertise, economy of effort, immunity from temptations and blackmail. These may affect large sections of the population in predominantly the same way. But here one may also expect a degree of individual variation. The authority of the state may be greater over some individuals than over others, depending on their personal circumstances.[19]

Mistakes That Serve No Purpose

Having dispensed with some preliminary worries about the instrumental argument for authority, we can now turn to what I believe to be a more serious problem.

19. Raz, *Morality of Freedom*, 100.

Let's return to the example of our state official, O. We assume that O's case is one where the conditions of the normal justification thesis are met—that is, O can best comply with his duty to serve citizens by taking the directives of his superiors as authoritatively binding rather than deliberating about the first-order reasons himself, case by case. On balance, better results will be produced if O follows orders. But although O can produce better results overall by following this strategy, it's not true that in each and every instance the best results will be produced if O simply follows orders. Sometimes O's superiors make mistakes—sometimes they direct O to do something that is unjust, a violation of some person's rights. If O follows the order in this case, O does not produce better results, but rather makes things go much worse. How can O be justified in following this order, when doing so serves no purpose, and indeed makes things worse?

The proponent of the instrumental argument for authority claims to have answered this question. Because, in general, O can best comply with his obligations to others by taking his superiors' directives as binding, he has to do this in each case, including the cases where O's superiors err. If O started deciding for himself whether or not to obey in each individual instance, he would no longer be doing what will, in the long run, be best for those whom he is meant to serve. This is why O is justified in obeying the mistaken directive.[20]

But this response conflates two separate questions about O's conduct. First, there is the question of what general strategy or disposition O ought to develop and cultivate toward his superior's orders. Second, there is the question of whether O acts permissibly when he obeys the mistaken directive. Suppose we grant that the answer to the first question is that O ought to develop and cultivate the attitude of obedience toward his superior's directives. It does not follow that the answer to the second question is that O acts permissibly in obeying the mistaken directive. The reasons why O should cultivate and develop the attitude of obedience are

20. For this response to the worry, see Raz, *Morality of Freedom*, 61.

instrumental—it's because doing so brings about better results. But these instrumental reasons are absent in the case of the mistaken directive: obeying this directive is not instrumentally useful, and so there's no instrumental value in carrying it out, but there is a very good reason not to carry it out. O thus lacks a justification for obeying the mistaken directive.

At first glance, this seems puzzling. How, after all, can we say that O is justified in cultivating the attitude of obedience in general, while simultaneously insisting that he lacks a justification for obeying in a given instance? But on reflection, the puzzle disappears. There's a difference between justifying a rule or policy, and justifying an act. Consider a more mundane example. You've learned from experience that it's generally not a good idea to let your children have anything sweet to eat after 7 p.m. If they eat after this time they sometimes have too much energy to go to bed and they sometimes get stomach aches that prevent them from sleeping. So you have a general policy that you won't give sweet things to eat after 7 p.m. But suppose one evening one of your kids is very upset, almost inconsolable, about something that happened at school and you guess correctly that letting them have a late-night ice cream might really help to cheer them up and calm them down before bed. Suppose also that in this instance none of the negative side effects of eating ice cream will eventuate. You have a good justification for the policy: in the long run following the policy brings the best results. But in this instance you have a good justification for not following it: you can bring about good consequences without any negative consequence. You shouldn't follow a rule that has an instrumental justification when, in a given instance, following it doesn't do any good.

This point is familiar from the literature on rule consequentialism. Rule consequentialists are accused of being guilty of *rule worship*—insisting we are obligated to follow a rule even when doing so doesn't deliver the promised good consequences. A structurally similar point applies to those who argue that the instrumental account of authority can justify obedience even in cases where the authority issues a mistaken directive. O has a good instrumental justification for adopting the general policy of treating his superior's directives as authoritatively binding. But if in a given instance he correctly believes a directive is unjust, he doesn't have an instrumental justification for obeying the mistaken directive. To hold otherwise is to be guilty of something like rule worship.

The instrumental argument for political authority thus doesn't vindicate the conclusion that there is a justification for obedience in cases where directives are mistakes that will not bring about the desired results. It thus does not provide an explanation of legitimate injustice.

Replies

Let's consider two possible replies on behalf of the instrumental argument for authority. First, proponents of the instrumental argument might help themselves to a response similar to that which rule consequentialists sometimes deploy when confronted by the rule worship objection. They might claim that what the instrumental argument in fact justifies is a more fine-grained policy than one of simple obedience in all cases where the normal justification thesis obtains. Perhaps when the normal justification thesis is met, the policy that our state official O should adopt is something more like: "treat my superiors' directives as authoritatively binding—as excluding and taking the place of my own deliberations—unless I happen to know, or at the very least am extremely confident, that the directive is unjust, in which case I should not obey." This more fine-grained policy apparently allows the instrumental argument to reach more intuitively plausible results. In cases where O knows, or is extremely confident, that a directive is unjust, surely it is plausible that he should disobey it? But in the absence of such knowledge or such a high degree of confidence, it is surely plausible to suppose that he ought to obey his superiors. Of course, some of these directives might be mistaken too, but since O isn't confident about this, he has an instrumental justification for obedience. We thus still get an explanation of legitimate injustice, but its scope is narrower and more intuitively plausible.

This reply, however, faces at least two problems. To begin, by making O's policy of obedience more fine-grained, we risk losing some of the instrumental benefits of the authority relation. O cannot simply obey directives without worrying about the content of the directives; he must now assess each directive and be sure it doesn't cross the threshold where he's sufficiently confident it is an error. Not only is this more burdensome for O; it also introduces the possibility of a new type of error: cases where O makes a mistake and disobeys a directive that was not an error. If O's confidence threshold for disobedience is set too low, we will entirely undermine the instrumental benefits of the relation of authority. But if we set the threshold too high, the account will end up with too many cases where O is reasonably sure a directive is unjust, it is in fact unjust, and yet O is apparently justified in obeying the directive. The proponent of this version of the instrumental argument needs to show that there is a sweet spot in between these outcomes, a policy of obedience that gives O just enough leeway to avoid the most intuitively clear cases where disobedience seems justified, without giving him so much leeway that we lose the instrumental benefits of the relation of authority. I am skeptical that such a sweet spot exists for many real cases of political officials.

There's a much more serious problem with the proposal, however. Regardless of where we set O's confidence threshold for disobedience, this doesn't avoid the original objection in those cases where O is, allegedly, duty-bound to follow the directive, but the directive is mistaken. There is still no instrumental justification for O obeying this mistaken directive. Doing so does not deliver any instrumental benefits, but it does result in injustice. There is thus no good reason for O to obey in these cases. The proposal has narrowed the range of such cases by giving O some latitude for disobedience, but that doesn't solve the more fundamental problem: the fact that there's a good instrumental justification for O to adopt a policy of obedience—no matter how fine-grained—does not suffice to show that O is justified in obeying in a given instance where the directive is mistaken.

Let's therefore turn to a second possible reply on behalf of the instrumentalist. The instrumentalist might grant that, specifically in those cases where O has sufficient evidence that a directive is unjust, he lacks a sufficient justification for obedience. There will thus be some cases where the instrumental argument for authority breaks down. But in many cases O may have no evidence that a directive is mistaken. When O has no, or little, evidence to suggest that a directive is mistaken, then he has a justification—the general instrumental benefits gained by treating his superiors as an authority—for obeying the directive, and no good reason to disobey. This is true even if the directive is in fact mistaken. We can thus still explain how legitimate injustice is sometime possible. Whenever O lacks sufficient evidence that a directive is mistaken, all that remains for O, in terms of his reasons for action, are the general instrumental benefits of accepting the relation of authority, and thus O has a justification for obeying even though sometimes he will be acting unjustly in doing so.

This reply, however, assumes a controversial thesis about justifications and reasons for action. It assumes that O's justifications and reasons for action are determined relative to O's evidence: what we have in a previous chapter called an evidence-relative standard. It assumes that O only has good reasons to disregard directives when he has sufficient evidence the directive is mistaken. But, of course, sometimes O will not have evidence that a directive is mistaken, even though the directive is in fact unjust. Those who hold that reasons for action and moral obligation should be understood relative to the facts, and not relative to the agent's evidence, will thus protest that O does have a compelling reason to disobey, regardless of his evidence. So one difficulty with this reply is that it commits the proponent of the instrumental argument to a controversial position about reasons and moral obligation.[21]

But let's set that issue aside. The more fundamental problem is that once we have adopted the evidence-relative standard, we end up with a very different, and less plausible, picture of practical authority than the instrumental picture with which we started. There will be many circumstances in which state officials are evidence-relative justified in acting but the normal justification thesis, as standardly understood, is not satisfied. For example, someone may have provided O with manufactured evidence that makes it reasonable for O to conclude that the normal justification thesis is satisfied, though as a matter of fact it is not. In this case O does not best comply with the fact-relative reasons that apply to him by obeying his superior's directives, but he does have an evidence-relative justification for treating his superiors as a genuine authority. This shows, I think, how implausible it is to build an instrumental account of authority in evidence-relative terms. If the purpose of having the relation of authority is its instrumental value—the benefits that it delivers—then it doesn't make much sense to focus on the subject's evidence-relative reasons, since those reasons might be unconnected with any actual benefits and burdens his compliance yields. We don't have a compelling interest in submitting to an authority so that we can better comply with our evidence-relative reasons, or not at least when those reasons depart from the fact-relative reasons. As a result, I think we can

---

21. It's also noteworthy that this position is one that Raz rejects. See, for example, Raz, *Engaging Reason*, ch. 2. To be clear, a person's ignorance of the facts might sometimes bear on her reasons for action (e.g., if I have a fact-relative reason to Φ but I am ignorant about how to Φ, I have a genuine reason to learn the information that will enable me to Φ). But this point does not defuse the objection. The instrumental view under consideration is one that supposes that the normal justification thesis obtains whenever the subject lacks sufficient evidence the authority is mistaken. But since an authority's directives might deliver no instrumental benefits under these conditions, it remains mysterious how there could nevertheless be genuine instrumental reasons to do what the authority directs.

dismiss this second reply in defense of the instrumental account of authority.

Conclusion

In this chapter we have focused on the idea that relations of political authority might be vindicated on instrumental grounds. In particular, we've examined a view on which political institutions have practical authority over subjects when, and because, those institutions enable subjects to better comply with their duties and obligations. As I emphasized, there is a lot to be said for this picture of political authority. It starts from the appealing view that those who govern gain their rightful authority by virtue of their capacity to serve the governed effectively. It promises to explain an apparently constitutive feature of political relations: namely, the power to issue commands and the duty to obey. It also seems to have the right sort of scope: it will deny political legitimacy to regimes, such as tyrannical regimes or kleptocracies, that we intuitively deem illegitimate, without making the attainment of political legitimacy too difficult for the imperfect regimes that govern many of us.

The instrumental argument for authority also appears to solve the puzzle of legitimate injustice. But this appearance, I argued, is illusory. There's a gap between the instrumental value of an institution or a rule, and the particular acts that officials are directed to perform. The general instrumental value of the relation of authority doesn't provide a justification for following unjust directives.

Although I have focused on Raz's service conception of authority specifically, any instrumental account of political authority or legitimacy will be confronted by the same problem. The fact that an institution delivers instrumental benefits relative to feasible alternatives may show that it's better to have that institution, compared to those alternatives. It shows that we have instrumental reasons to keep or preserve the institution. But appeals to the instrumental value of an institution do not suffice to justify the authority of each particular directive or the permissibility of acting in accordance with a particular directive. Following Niko Kolodny, we can call this general difficulty for instrumental views the *bridging problem*.[22] Theories that appeal to the instrumental epistemic benefits of democratic institutions also face the bridging problem.[23] The problem is, in my view, an insurmountable one for all purely instrumental accounts of political institutions. In the next chapter we will thus turn to consider theories of political legitimacy grounded in non-instrumental considerations, in particular the non-instrumental value of equality.

22. Kolodny, "Rule Over None II," 291.
23. For different versions of such views, see Estlund, *Democratic Authority*; Landemore, *Democratic Reason*.

5

Democracy and Equality

THE PRECEDING chapter highlighted a problem for instrumental accounts of political authority. Such accounts are confronted by the bridging problem: they cannot explain why the general instrumental value of an institution delivers legitimacy to specific mistaken decisions of the institution that result in the imposition of an unjust law or the unjust enforcement of a law. There is no instrumental reason to follow directives that fail to deliver the promised instrumental benefits.

An obvious response to this problem is to consider whether our political institutions have non-instrumental value. If an institution has intrinsic or non-instrumental value, then even when the institution fails to deliver good outcomes, there is a non-instrumental reason to value what the institution does. This could be the sort of reason that won't face the bridging problem, and thus might more successfully resolve the puzzle of legitimate injustice.

This chapter focuses on a family of such views that I will refer to as *democratic egalitarianism*. These views are united in their appeal to some egalitarian property of democratic decision-making that is claimed to be non-instrumentally valuable or just. Thomas Christiano, for example, claims that "[d]emocratic decision-making enables us all to see that we are being treated as equals despite disagreements as long as we take into account the facts of judgment and the interests that accompany them. Because democratic decision-making realizes public equality in this way, and there is pervasive disagreement on its outcomes, it is intrinsically just."[1] Laura Valentini similarly claims that "since thick reasonable disagreements are pervasive in our political world, liberals should value democracy first and foremost as an intrinsic requirement of justice."[2] In a somewhat different vein, Niko Kolodny argues that "what justifies democracy [. . .] is that democracy is a particularly important constituent of a society in which people are related to one another as social equals, as opposed to social inferiors or superiors."[3] Daniel Viehoff also defends an account of democracy that focuses on egalitarian relationships, "according to which egalitarian procedures have authority because, by obeying them, we can avoid acting on certain considerations that must be excluded from our intrinsically valuable egalitarian relationships."[4]

Although democratic egalitarians each develop subtle and distinctive arguments, the arguments share a common structure. They identify some property of democratic institutions that is held to be non-instrumentally valuable. That value is then alleged to ground the authority and/or legitimacy of democratic decisions. Because the authority or legitimacy of democratic decisions is not primarily tied to the outcomes produced by those decisions, but rather to some non-instrumental property of the decision-making, democratic egalitarians may be better placed to explain the phenomenon of legitimate injustice. If laws emerge from appropriately democratic procedures, the non-instrumental value of equality may yet explain why such laws remain legitimate.

Accounts of democratic authority rooted in the non-instrumental value of equality are appealing beyond their potential to explain the puzzle of legitimate injustice. Many people's commitment to democratic institutions is not contingent on those institutions being the best mechanism for delivering benefits.

1. Christiano, *Constitution of Equality*, 76.
2. Valentini, "Justice, Disagreement," 178.
3. Kolodny, "Rule Over None II," 317.
4. Viehoff, "Democratic Equality," 340.

Many of us believe that we have reasons to respect the outcome of the democratic process even when we are confident the process is not going to deliver the correct result. We think of democratic decision-making as constituting a fair way to resolve our political disagreements, and the fairness of the process is surely relevant to understanding the alleged authority and legitimacy of democratic decisions. Theories that focus on the non-instrumental value of democratic institutions also seem well suited to explain the widely held view that non-democratic political institutions are always, at least in some way, defective, regardless of how well such institutions might perform in terms of outcomes.

The chapter begins by distinguishing different versions of democratic egalitarianism. Some contend that democratic institutions are essential to the public manifestation of equal respect. Others construe democratic institutions as constitutive of the realization of egalitarian or non-hierarchical social relations. I identify the common features and advantages of this family of theories. I then consider some preliminary challenges to such theories: for example, difficulties they have explaining the connection between democracy's non-instrumental value and its alleged authority or legitimacy, or explaining the limited scope of democratic authority. More importantly, I proceed to argue that democratic egalitarianism cannot successfully solve the puzzle of legitimate injustice. The central problem is that there is no compelling way to explain why the non-instrumental value of democracy should reliably trump or outweigh the importance of averting substantive injustice. I consider some potential responses on behalf of democratic egalitarians, but argue that these responses are unlikely to succeed. The chapter concludes with some general remarks on the relationship between democracy and the non-instrumental value of equality.

Justice and Democratic Equality

This section and the following one briefly survey some theories of democracy that explain the authority or legitimacy of democratic institutions primarily by appeal to equality and its non-instrumental value. The survey will not be comprehensive—there are too many views that fall within this broad camp. Instead, I divide these theories into two sub-categories—justice-based, and relational—and discuss some illustrative examples within each category. The focus in this section is specifically on justice-based theories of democratic equality. These theories emphasize the way the value of justice itself generates a requirement to make our political decisions in a broadly egalitarian fashion via a democratic process. Let's look at three illustrative examples of this sort of view.

Christiano and Public Equality

On Christiano's view, the value of democracy lies primarily in the fact that democratic institutions constitute what he calls *public equality*. As he puts it, "it must not only be the case that people are treated as equals, they must be able to see that they are treated as equals."[5] People must be able, at least in principle, to see that their interests are being equally advanced or counted equally. According to Christiano, this conception of public equality takes priority in theorizing about justice because the value of justice substantially underdetermines what social rules we ought to adopt. Because justice does not, on its own, dictate the adoption of a particular set of rules, what becomes most significant is that we are each publicly treated as equals given our disagreements about how our political institutions and laws ought to be arranged: "the first duty of equality is to treat persons publicly as equals."[6] Being publicly treated as an equal is, for Christiano, crucial in part because it is a precondition of being able to pursue many of our other interests.

The only way to realize public equality in politics, according to Christiano, is via democratic decision-making:

> Democratic decision-making is the unique way to publicly embody equality in collective decision-making under the circumstances of pervasive conscientious disagreement in which we

5. Christiano, *Constitution of Equality*, 46.
6. Christiano, *Constitution of Equality*, 250–51.

find ourselves. Democratic decision-making enables us all to see that we are being treated as equals despite disagreements as long as we take into account the facts of judgment and the interests that accompany them.[7]

For Christiano, it's not merely that democratic decision-making realizes the non-instrumental value of public equality; it also justifies the authority of democratic decisions, including the right to issue commands, and the corresponding capacity to generate obligations to obey those commands: obligations that are typically not overridden by other considerations.[8] His argument for this position is complex, but depends crucially on the following two claims: (1) only a state that accords equal respect to differing opinions can be legitimate (i.e., possess the right to rule); and (2) only states with democratic forms of decision-making accord differing opinions the requisite form of equal respect.

Christiano thus begins with an egalitarian account of social justice and then argues that it grounds the authority and legitimacy of democratic political decisions.

Pettit on the Priority of Political Justice

Philip Pettit distinguishes between what he calls social and political justice.[9] Social justice, for Pettit, is "is something that the state provides for its people as the more or less passive beneficiaries of the system," whereas political justice "is something that [the state] delivers for its people in their role as active citizens: that is, as members of the society who ought presumptively to share in setting the terms on which their state acts."[10] The former concerns questions of the rightful allocation of things like resources, legal

---

7. Christiano, *Constitution of Equality*, 75–76.
8. Christiano, *Constitution of Equality*, 244.
9. Pettit, "Justice."
10. Pettit, "Justice," 10.

liberties, educational and economic opportunities. The latter concerns questions of how we are to make our political decisions.

Pettit makes his argument for democracy using building blocks or assumptions drawn from theories of social justice. To begin, he notes that all plausible theories of social justice share the disposition of forbearance: that is, such theories are presented "in the forum of public debate as a theory offered for the consideration of others, not as a blueprint to be coercively implemented, regardless of people's attitudes towards it."[11] There may be many different reasons grounding this disposition of forbearance, but the disposition, in combination with pervasive disagreement about justice, establishes the need for an account of political justice: a theory as to how political decisions are to be made amongst citizens who are, from the point of view of social justice, regarded as equals.

Pettit then notes that since all plausible theories of social justice are offered in the spirit of recommendations to the public, there's a background presupposition that the audience for such theories is competent to understand, assess, and act on those recommendations. From this, he argues we can derive a more determinate form that just political decision-making ought to take. It should be one "in which each citizen, each member of the public, is invited to participate in a deliberative manner," on an equal footing.[12] Some form of democratic process is thus entailed by basic features of all plausible theories of social justice.

More strongly, Pettit argues that political justice requires robust democratic control. This follows from the fact that justice requires modal robustness.[13] Justice hasn't been properly achieved when its realization is fragile because modest changes in empirical circumstances would unravel it. For example, we aren't inclined to think the basic structure of society is just if the protection of a minority group's civil liberties depends on the good will of a few

11. Pettit, "Justice," 13.
12. Pettit, "Justice," 19.
13. Pettit, "Justice," 25–30.

political leaders, or is sensitive to small demographic changes. A just basic structure must be sufficiently robust across a range of close possible worlds. In particular, it must not be contingent on people's continuing benevolence toward those with whom they disagree or of whom they disapprove. The upshot, Pettit argues, is that the commitment to democratic decision-making is not dispensable, even via the democratic process itself. Democratic control over our collective decisions must be ongoing, and competent adults cannot be excluded from this political process. Our rights to political participation on roughly equal terms are not themselves conditional on democratic approval.

Even more strongly, Pettit argues that political justice has priority over social justice. He notes that unlike our fundamental rights to political participation—which are not conditional on democratic approval—claims of social justice are presented as conditional upon democratic approval. In these ways, Pettit presents an argument for the authority of democratic institutions that is rooted in the nature of egalitarian theories of social justice.

Valentini and Equal Respect

Laura Valentini also develops an account of democracy grounded in a political conception of equality: in particular, a conception of equal respect. According to Valentini, equal respect entails that our political principles and rules should satisfy a condition of mutual justifiability; we should each be able, in some sense, to recognize and accept the reasons in favor of the rules that purport to have authority over our collective life.[14]

How is mutual justifiability possible in the face of sharp and pervasive disagreement about so many political questions? For Valentini, the answer to this question depends on the type of disagreement, which can be distinguished on two dimensions. First,

---

14. Valentini, "Justice, Disagreement," 178.

she distinguishes between *thick* and *thin* disagreements. In the case of thin disagreements, we advance conflicting claims about justice, but we agree about the truth conditions that would settle our disagreement.[15] For example, we might hold differing views about whether justice requires the abolition of private schools for children, but we might agree that our dispute turns on the question of whether abolishing private schooling has any measurable effect on improving social mobility for the least advantaged. On the other hand, there are thick disagreements; these are disagreements where not only do we advance conflicting claims about justice, but we also do not agree on the truth conditions that would settle our disagreements. Disagreements about fundamental political values would seem to be of this type. For example, disagreements between those who think religious considerations are central to political morality and those who deny the existence of such reasons at all are thick disagreements.

Second, there is the difference between *reasonable* and *unreasonable* disagreements.[16] According to Valentini, disagreements are reasonable when there is no "obviously" correct answer, whereas a disagreement is unreasonable when some parties to the dispute are "obviously" mistaken. Disputes between prioritarians and egalitarians about distributive ethics would presumably qualify as reasonable disagreements, whereas disputes between racists and non-racists would presumably qualify as unreasonable.

With these distinctions in hand, Valentini defends the conclusion that democratic decision-making is what's required by equal respect in cases of thick, reasonable disagreement. Equal respect does not require the granting of equal weight to the views of those who are obviously or demonstrably mistaken. Nor does equal respect require democratic decision-making in cases where the disagreement is thin rather than thick, since in these cases all parties

15. Valentini, "Justice, Disagreement," 182.
16. Valentini, "Justice, Disagreement," 184–85.

to the dispute agree on the truth conditions that would settle their disagreement, and thus there's nothing disrespectful about deferring to those with the relevant expertise to resolve those disputes. In cases of thick, reasonable disagreement, however, "none of the parties involved can be accused of being irrational or obviously mistaken. To that extent, their points of view merit being taken seriously," and the only appropriate way to do this is via the egalitarian procedures of democratic decision-making.[17]

The theories developed by Christiano, Pettit, and Valentini share a common structure. Each begins with some fundamental claims about the nature of egalitarian justice, and those claims, when combined with some further assumptions, are meant to establish that our major political decisions must be made democratically, and that those decisions can be authoritative and legitimate even if they are, in some sense, substantively mistaken.

Democracy and Egalitarian Relations

Let's now turn to our second family of egalitarian theories. These theories begin with claims about the non-instrumental value of standing in certain kinds of non-hierarchical, or egalitarian, relations with others.

Kolodny's Claim Against Inferiority

According to Kolodny, we each have "a claim against standing in a *relation of inferiority* to another person: against being subordinated to another, or set beneath them in a social hierarchy."[18] There are three main ways, according to Kolodny, that some people can stand in relations of inferiority to others: (1) inequality of power, (2) inequality of de facto authority, and (3) inequality of consideration. When two or more people are unequal in any of these

17. Valentini, "Justice, Disagreement," 185.
18. Kolodny, *Pecking Order*, 87.

ways, and those persons also stand in some kind of relationship with each other, that relationship is a hierarchical one, and as such, it violates at least someone's claim against being in a relation of inferiority.[19]

Why is it bad for people to stand in relations of inferiority? The explanation Kolodny provides is inductive. He considers a series of widely held claims about our social and political life. These claims include: claims against being subjected to the coercion of even a reasonably decent state; claims against corrupt use of an office; claims against certain forms of discrimination; claims to equal treatment; and claims against certain illiberal interferences. Kolodny argues that the standard ways of trying to vindicate these claims do not succeed, or are at least incomplete. But these claims can, he argues, be successfully explained if we posit that there is a claim against standing in relations of inferiority.

Importantly for our purposes, Kolodny also argues that the commonplace assumption that we ought to make our political decisions democratically is best vindicated by appeal to the importance of not standing in hierarchical relations. Democratic forms of decision-making are required not for instrumental reasons—not because those institutions are most likely to promote our interests or protect our freedom—but rather because only by giving each person an equal say in political decisions can we avoid standing in relations of inferiority to others.

---

19. Kolodny in fact qualifies this claim. On his account, the inequalities in question do not necessarily violate the claim against being in a relation of inferiority if there are "tempering" factors that justify the inequality. These tempering factors include: that the relationship is a one-off encounter; that the inequalities are limited in time, place, or context; that the inequalities are limited in their content; that the inequalities are escapable at little or no cost or difficulty; that an inequality in consideration is merited or deserved; that the inequalities are not final but can be appealed or overturned; and that the inegalitarian relationship might be offset by an egalitarian relationship in a different context. See Kolodny, *Pecking Order*, 97–98.

Viehoff and Non-Subjection

Like Kolodny, Viehoff justifies democratic institutions in terms of the value of egalitarian relations.[20] When persistent conflicts of interest and persistent disagreements about moral rights are pervasive, Viehoff argues, it is almost certainly to everyone's benefit to coordinate in producing a single set of rules to which everyone is required to give priority, even when those rules are very far from the rules anyone sees as optimal. To achieve this kind of coordination, an adjudicator must have authority to determine individuals' rights and duties. For Viehoff, the authority of political institutions thus lies in their capacity to serve as an effective arbitrator. But many different individuals or institutions could potentially play the role of adjudicator, and so the mere need for such an adjudicator can't ground the authority of democratic institutions in particular. Democratic institutions are required, on Viehoff's account, insofar as relationships between citizens are regulated by an ideal of non-subjection.[21] Relationships satisfy the condition of non-subjection when none of the parties involved in the relationship use arbitrary inequalities in power to effectively determine the rules that govern the relationship. A spouse, for example, who uses the greater financial security he would enjoy in the event of divorce to tilt the norms of the marriage in his favor creates a relationship with his spouse where non-subjection is not realized. Viehoff argues that democratic political institutions are constitutive of securing relationships—both in the public and private sphere—characterized by non-subjection.

Although there are many points of similarity, Kolodny's and Viehoff's views also differ in some important respects. On Kolodny's view, the key to understanding relational equality is to see it as the absence of various forms of social hierarchy. Caste systems are the paradigmatic obstacles to this kind of relational equality.

20. Viehoff, "Democratic Equality."
21. Viehoff, "Democratic Equality," 354–59.

On Viehoff's view, certain kinds of ideal egalitarian interpersonal relationships, such as friendships or the relationship between spouses, provide the correct picture of relational equality.

As Viehoff acknowledges, each model has different strengths and weaknesses.[22] Kolodny's focus on the absence of social hierarchy has the advantage of clearly mapping onto important aspects of our social and political life. There's no difficulty in understanding how, in principle, this conception of equality is relevant to the structure of our political institutions. Many forms of social organization that we now reject (feudalism or caste-based societies) seem wrong, at least in part, because they are constituted by objectionable social hierarchies. The disadvantage of this model, according to Viehoff, is that it fails to offer a persuasive case for the constitutive role of democratic institutions. Inegalitarian, non-democratic forms of governance need not create social hierarchies, so long as those who wield power are appropriately guided by the aim of serving the interests of those that they govern. The interpersonal relationships model, by contrast, offers a potentially better basis for the importance of egalitarian decision-making. Viehoff claims that the best versions of these types of interpersonal relationships are constituted, in part, by the parties having an equal say over decisions. The disadvantage of this model is that it may not be clear why our civic relations should be modeled on anything like the interpersonal relationships we have with our friends and spouses.

Democratic Egalitarianism: Advantages

The views canvassed in the preceding two sections share a number of appealing features. First, grounding the value and authority of democracy in equality coheres with a commonsense view about democratic institutions. Many people, if pressed to explain why we should make our political decisions democratically, are likely

---

22. Viehoff, "Power and Equality."

to reply that doing so is required as a matter of fairness or equality. When we cannot agree what to do, it's only fair to give each person an equal say about the outcome. The importance of giving each an equal say might be explained, at a deeper level, by the importance of equal respect, or the importance of avoiding relations of inferiority, but accounts of democratic authority that don't make essential reference to the importance of equal treatment will miss something widely seen as essential.

Second, and relatedly, democratic egalitarianism can readily explain the commonplace assumption that the value of democratic institutions cannot be reduced to their instrumental benefits. Many would reject the suggestion that democratic institutions should be replaced with a benevolent non-democratic ruling elite, even if that elite could outperform our democratic institutions in terms of outcomes.

Third, democratic egalitarianism can easily avoid a difficulty highlighted in the previous chapter that instrumental theories confront and have no easy way to overcome: the bridging problem. The problem, recall, is that the general instrumental value of an institution doesn't entail that any particular mistaken decision by that institution or its officials is legitimate or authoritative. There cannot be an instrumental reason to put up with decisions that deliver no instrumental benefits. Democratic egalitarianism doesn't face this worry. It holds that democratic decisions instantiate the value of equality. Thus, even when democratic decisions are substantively mistaken, there remains a compelling reason to accept the decisions as legitimate or authoritative.

Finally, democratic egalitarianism, in at least some of its guises, promises to resolve the puzzle of legitimate injustice. As we have seen, democratic egalitarianism is sometimes developed as an account of what justice entails with regard to our political decision-making. Democratic decisions are authoritative and legitimate, on this account, because they are the outcome of a process mandated by justice. Although some of our democratic decisions will be mistaken and thus substantively unjust, they remain procedurally just.

The phenomenon of legitimate injustice can thus apparently be explained without giving up any of the three claims that comprise our puzzle. If the just procedures for resolving (at least some of) our political disagreements take precedence over non-procedural justice, then substantively unjust decisions can be deemed legitimate without abandoning a version of the claim that justice is the first virtue of social institutions. Justice, on this picture, is multifaceted, and the inevitability of political disagreement means that sometimes the only way to give priority to justice is to prioritize the just procedures by which we address those disagreements.

Preliminary Challenges

But democratic egalitarianism is not without its own challenges. Suppose we are persuaded that there is intrinsic or non-instrumental value inherent in democratic decision-making—that some version of equal respect or egalitarian relations between persons in cases of political disagreement are realized through such processes. It does not automatically follow that democratic decisions are legitimate or authoritative. Further argument is required. Different versions of democratic egalitarianism answer this challenge in different ways. My point here is that we might accept the initial idea that democracy has non-instrumental value, while resisting further claims about the legitimacy or authority of democratic institutions.

A related challenge for democratic egalitarians is to explain how, if at all, the scope of democratic authority or legitimacy is limited. Even ardent defenders of democracy typically concede that the authority of democratic institutions is limited in scope— that some decisions or domains of social life are not appropriately subject to democratic control. Most of us, for example, believe that democratic majorities lack the right to issue or enforce laws concerning what religious doctrines people may accept, or prohibiting sex between consenting adults. The challenge for democratic egalitarians is to explain how the non-instrumental value of equality grounds the authority of some democratic decisions but not others in ways that track widely shared liberal ideas.

Democratic egalitarians must also show that the value or importance of equality requires recognizably democratic institutions. There is pressure from opposite directions. On the one hand, there are those who will argue that equality does not uniquely entail orthodox democratic institutions. Some will insist it is also consistent with sortition or lottocracy, or perhaps the requisite form of equality can be realized under anarchist or other non-governmental forms of social life. On the other hand, some may worry that modern democratic institutions—for example, representative democracy, whereby a voter's probability of being influential can vary greatly depending on her particular electoral district or constituency—do not in fact realize the relevant form of equal respect or egalitarian relations.[23] One may worry that egalitarianism properly construed will in fact require forms of collective decision-making (e.g., face-to-face deliberative forums where all citizens are present and equally situated) that likely aren't feasible in large societies with millions of residents.

I don't claim that any of the preceding challenges are insurmountable for proponents of democratic egalitarianism. But it is important to keep these challenges in view since, as we will see below, certain ways of addressing them can create further difficulties for these theories.

Deeper Challenges

Let's now return to our central question. Does democratic egalitarianism, in any of its forms, offer a satisfactory explanation of the relationship between justice and legitimacy? In particular, does it offer a compelling solution to the puzzle of legitimate injustice? Although the idea has been developed in different ways, all the

---

23. For a forceful expression of this worry, see Landa and Pevnick, *Representative Democracy*, ch. 4.

accounts we have canvassed share a common structure. They identify some property of democratic institutions that is held to be non-instrumentally valuable, and then claim that that value grounds the authority and legitimacy of democratic decisions.

I want to highlight a simple but significant worry about the common structure of the argument. Whatever property is identified as having non-instrumental value—the public manifestation of equality, equal respect, or relations of non-inferiority—it's a further question whether this value is sufficiently weighty to legitimize substantively unjust decisions in the range of cases where democratic institutions are typically deemed to possess authority and legitimacy. It's not obvious why we should believe that the non-instrumental value is likely—over a defined range of issues— to have greater weight or importance than avoiding substantive injustice. We can call this the *weighing problem*. This problem can be developed in a number of different ways.

First, even if democratic institutions are non-instrumentally valuable, without further explanation, this at most gives us a reason to use a democratic process, rather than some other process, when choosing amongst options that are not unjust. We need some compelling explanation of why democratic institutions should even in principle extend in scope to cover the imposition of unjust laws.[24]

Some democratic egalitarians do purport to provide such an explanation. Pettit, for example, argues that all plausible theories of social justice share the disposition of forbearance—that is, they are presented as recommendations to be enacted via an appropriate political process, not as claims to be enforced on dissenters in the absence of such a process. If that's the correct picture, then the scope of our democratic decision-making must by necessity include decisions between competing claims about justice, not all of which can be correct.

---

24. This worry is raised in Wellman, "Space Between."

I think we should be somewhat skeptical of Pettit's argument. Some claims advanced about social justice are not in fact advanced in the spirit of forbearance. Consider Rawls's theory of justice as fairness. Rawls famously asserts that each "person possesses an inviolability founded on justice that even the welfare of society as a whole cannot override," and that "in a just society the liberties of equal citizenship are taken as settled."[25] He later makes clear that the equal basic liberties are not being put forward as a recommendation—as something that needs to be ratified by a democratic process. Rather, they are to be constitutionally secured and thus put beyond the reach of the legislative process. His idea that at least certain core claims of social justice are non-negotiable and not conditional upon political approval is not idiosyncratic. That persons have certain rights—for example, against murder and assault, or claims to religious freedom and freedom of association— are widely believed to be pre-institutional. If so, those rights give rise to claims that can be forcefully defended regardless of whether they have been democratically sanctioned. If many claims of social justice are not advanced as mere recommendations awaiting political approval, it isn't clear why the scope of democratic decision-making should include such matters.

Valentini provides a different explanation as to why the scope of democratic decision-making must extend to include unjust errors. On her account, recall, in cases of thick, reasonable disagreement "none of the parties involved can be accused of being irrational or obviously mistaken."[26] Equal respect thus requires that such disagreements be handled democratically.

But it's unclear why equal respect always requires giving each an equal say in cases where no one is obviously mistaken. This conclusion seems most plausible in cases where we are trying to advance everyone's interests or projects (which vacation spot we should choose, for example), but there is disagreement about how to do

25. Rawls, *Theory of Justice*, 3.
26. Valentini, "Justice, Disagreement," 185.

so. It seems less plausible in cases where a majority seeks to define the rights of a minority against the minority's wishes. Suppose that a political community cannot agree about the limits on the right to free speech: the majority believes anti-Semitic hate speech is not protected by the right to free speech, but a minority (including those who seek to express such views) believe the right does extend to protect hate speech. It's not obvious, at least to me, that equal respect requires giving the majority the power to define the contours of this right. It seems at least as plausible to suppose that equal respect is best instantiated by non-democratically protecting a robust, content-independent right to freedom of speech for all, allowing only for familiar exceptions such as speech that is constitutive of a crime or speech threatening imminent harm. Such laws respect each person's agency and choices about what views to express and what views to engage with. Similar worries arise when we consider other disagreements: for example, about abortion, recreational drug use, or the permissibility of polygamous marriages.[27]

In sum, respect is complex and multifaceted. When there is reasonable disagreement about what to do, and none of the options involve infringing or defining anyone's rights, it is certainly plausible to suppose that equal respect requires giving people an equal say. But when the disagreement concerns options that may infringe or purport to define some people's rights, it is much less obvious that equal respect always requires giving people an equal say. Sometimes equal respect plausibly requires providing everyone with an equal sphere of liberty or independence, immune

27. Some democratic theorists may respond by insisting that having the judiciary, or some other non-majoritarian institution, serve as a check on what majorities can do is not non-democratic, but rather a constitutive part of the democratic process and vindicated by the value of equal respect. See, for example, Shiffrin, *Democratic Law*. But such a move doesn't seem available to Valentini, since the key feature of her view is that equal respect requires giving each person an equal say regarding reasonable, thick disagreements about justice. She thus cannot place such disagreements beyond the limits of democratic majorities.

from majoritarian decision-making, where each can make their own choices.

But even if we assume this worry about the scope of democratic decision-making can be addressed, the very same feature of democratic institutions that is held to be non-instrumentally valuable can also be undermined by the democratic enactment of unjust laws; and this is a problem for all democratic egalitarians, not just Valentini.[28] Egalitarian relationships can, for example, be threatened not only by a failure to respect egalitarian decision procedures, but also by inegalitarian distributions of income and wealth, or inegalitarian access to important medical services. Similarly, though we may fail to show equal respect to persons when we fail to respect democratic decisions, we may also fail to show equal respect to persons when we unjustly imprison them for possessing recreational drugs, or when we unjustly deny them a fair opportunity to earn a decent income. Indeed, it seems clear that egalitarian relationships or equal respect can be more seriously threatened by some substantively unjust laws than by failures to adhere to a democratic process. If someone manages to prevent my ballot from being counted, I may suffer some form of disrespect, but the disrespect I suffer is surely small by comparison with the disrespect suffered by someone who is unjustly imprisoned for years for possessing recreational drugs, or the would-be immigrant who is unjustly detained at the border and denied a life-changing opportunity in a new country.

Democratic egalitarians thus face an unpalatable choice. Either they can, implausibly, deny that the relevant non-instrumental value is ever imperiled by unjust democratic decisions, or they can concede that unjust laws sometimes gravely threaten the relevant non-instrumental value—the very same value that is alleged to explain democratic authority and legitimacy. But this concession looks fatal for theories that aspire to explain the fairly broad scope that

28. This point is pressed in Stemplowska and Swift, "Dethroning Democratic Legitimacy," 18–19.

democratic institutions are widely believed to possess with regard to making legitimate decisions. If egalitarian relationships can be threatened by unjust decisions, for example, then surely we should not conclude that democratic decisions are—over some defined scope—authoritative and legitimate by virtue of instantiating egalitarian relationships among citizens. Instead, we must assess each decision on a case-by-case basis to determine how egalitarian relationships can be best protected. Sometimes this will require adhering to the results of the democratic process, but sometimes it will require disregarding those results in order to avert serious substantive injustices that threaten such relationships.[29]

Let's return to the first horn of the dilemma. Suppose we grant for the sake of argument the (implausible) idea that the non-instrumental value realized by democratic institutions is distinct, and thus never threatened by the imposition of a substantively unjust law. The question of its relative importance remains open. What arguments, if any, could be advanced to establish that, as a general principle, the non-instrumental value of democracy takes precedence over the importance of averting all the types of ordinary substantive injustice that democratic majorities can and do commit?

Christiano is the democratic egalitarian who most explicitly takes up this challenge. He claims that

> the duty to treat others as equals by respecting and obeying the democratic decisions pre-empts or at least normally outweighs the other duties a citizen has. It does this because the duty is grounded in public equality while the others are merely grounded in equality and because the duties of equality precede all other duties. The preemption occurs because it is precisely in the context of disagreement on the substantive requirements of equality for law and policy that the principle of public equality requires democratic decision-making. The principle of public equality then directs us to subordinate one's

---

29. This is, broadly, the position defended by Stemplowska and Swift in "Dethroning Democratic Legitimacy."

conception of equality and its implications for law and policy
to democratic equality. So once a democratic decision has been
made that does not violate public equality one must act on the
basis of the decision and put aside one's own particular conception of equality at least as a guide to action.[30]

There are several difficulties with this position. First, it's unclear
why democratic decisions should preempt an individual's judgment about what justice requires. Christiano's account of democratic authority is not grounded in the capacity of democratic
institutions reliably to make better decisions than individual citizens, and so a given citizen has no epistemic reason to subordinate
her judgment to the decision of the majority. To explain preemp-
tion, Christiano must insist that the nature of public equality is
such that it always preempts facts about injustice that are not
explicable in terms of public equality. But why this should be so
remains puzzling. Many of the issues over which democratic majorities must legislate are topics where grave injustice is possible,
and where lives are sometimes at stake (e.g., war, abortion, eutha-
nasia, the death penalty). I find it difficult to believe that if the
democratic majority errs, and imposes laws that will result in unjust deaths, the fact that some people are being unjustly killed is
entirely preempted by or subordinated to the public equality of
the decision-making process.

A further difficulty arises when we consider disagreements
about the requirements of public equality. Suppose, for example,
that I think public equality does not require the extension of
voting rights to currently incarcerated felons, whereas you believe public equality does require voting rights for such felons.
This disagreement about the political process seems no less reasonable or intractable than many of the disagreements about
substantive matters of justice. But then how should such disagreements be resolved? There's an obvious difficulty if we

30. Christiano, *Constitution of Equality*, 254–55.

answer "democratically," since the dispute concerns what counts as appropriately "democratic."

Even if we set this difficulty aside, there's a further problem. Christiano is clear that we do not have to defer to democratic decisions that violate the requirements of public equality.[31] Suppose, for the moment, that my position on the voting rights of felons is mistaken because it is inconsistent with public equality. Christiano ought to conclude that if my view wins out via an apparently fair democratic process, this decision lacks authority and legitimacy. That's a surprising result. Many of our disagreements about the scope and limits of rights to political participation seem as reasonable and intractable as the other disagreements that surely ought to be handled via the democratic process. Suppose Christiano concedes that disagreements such as the one about the voting rights of felons ought to be resolved, somehow, democratically, and that such a resolution would be authoritative and legitimate. This concession implies that even disagreements about the nature of public equality must be resolved democratically. It's not clear what justifies this conclusion. It cannot be the value of public equality itself, since our disagreement concerns the requirements of public equality—you believe my position with regard to incarcerated felons violates public equality, whereas I believe that yours does. However our disagreement gets resolved, one of us is likely to insist the requirements of public equality were not met via the process of democratic resolution.

The more fundamental problem is that we cannot bootstrap the authority and legitimacy of the democratic process. The democratic process cannot be the source of its own authority and legitimacy: there must be some independent value or set of considerations that grounds the authority or legitimacy of democratic institutions. But Christiano's account makes it difficult to see how this could work. The value of public equality is presented as something that inheres

---

31. Christiano, *Constitution of Equality*, 260–61.

in the democratic process, not as a procedure-independent standard by which democratic institutions can be assessed.

To sum up, democratic egalitarians explain the authority and legitimacy of democratic decisions by appeal to the non-instrumental value of those decisions. But however we construe this non-instrumental value, we are confronted by the problem of how this value should be weighed or ranked relative to other considerations. How does the non-instrumentalist explain why the scope of democratic decisions should ever extend to include substantively unjust decisions? Even if we can answer this question, why should this value reliably trump or outweigh the substantive injustices that democratic majorities can and do commit, especially in light of the fact that the very same non-instrumental value alleged to justify democratic authority and legitimacy is often imperiled by unjust, but democratically authorized, laws? I've suggested that democratic egalitarians have yet to provide compelling answers to these questions.

Defending Democracy?

What might democratic egalitarians say in response to these worries? One potential response would be to concede that the non-instrumental value of democratic institutions provides a merely pro tanto reason in favor of the permissibility of enforcing democratic legislation. Because it is merely pro tanto, it must always be weighed up against other considerations. Thus, we cannot assume that democratic laws over some defined scope are legitimate and that state officials have, within that scope, rights against harmful interference when carrying out their democratically authorized duties. These are questions that can—as Stemplowska and Swift suggest—only be determined on a case-by-case basis.[32]

But this concessive response is not one that democratic egalitarians are inclined to make. As we've seen, democratic egalitarians

32. Stemplowska and Swift, "Dethroning Democratic Legitimacy."

seek to vindicate fairly general claims about the scope of democratic decision-making; they aim to establish that democratic legislation is typically both authoritative and legitimate, and some—such as Pettit and Christiano—are very explicit that democratic decisions can remain legitimate and authoritative even when they are substantively unjust. In the preceding section we looked at how particular democratic theorists address the worries about democracy's scope and the relative importance of its non-instrumental value in the face of substantive injustice. I now want to take a step back from the details of those arguments and consider some general strategies available to democratic egalitarians.

Consider first the worry about scope: why should the scope of democratic decision-making include substantively unjust decisions? The most plausible and obvious answer appeals to what is feasible or realistic. Deep, intractable disagreement about politics characterizes every modern political society. Given the pervasive nature of our political disagreements, we lack the ability reliably to design democratic institutions whose scope is limited in such a way as to exclude all substantively unjust decisions. We do not agree about what justice permits, prohibits, and requires. A model of democracy whose scope excludes substantively unjust decisions would have to be indexed to a specific theory of justice. Each theory of justice would thus have a different conception of the scope of democratic decision-making. This, of course, is of no help in addressing our practical problem. We require a method of political decision-making that adjudicates disagreements between rival views about justice. A realistic model of democracy must allow for the fact of pervasive disagreement about justice, and thus a realistic model of democracy cannot include a clause that deems substantively unjust decisions to be outside the scope of democratic decision-making.

This appeal to feasibility or realism, however, does not explain the legitimacy or authority of democratic decisions that are unjust. From the fact that we are unable reliably to design democratic institutions that will not make unjust errors, it does not follow (at least not without further premises) that when our institutions do err, those errors can be permissibly enforced by state officials, or that those officials have claims against harmful interference. Consider an analogy.[33] Suppose we are deliberating about whether to launch a military campaign to defend an ally from an aggressor. We know that wars always involve injustice. Even if we never deliberately target noncombatants, many noncombatants will be killed or harmed during the conflict. And we know there's a very high chance some of our troops may violate the laws of war and commit atrocities. It's unrealistic to expect to conduct a war that involves no injustice. It clearly doesn't follow from this fact that the injustices our side commits during the war are permissible, nor that the combatants who commit these injustices have rights against defensive harm. Knowing that we will commit injustice in the future can hardly suffice to render doing so permissible. This would be, to modify a Rawlsian phrase, to make our political theory realistic in the wrong way.

What it is feasible or realistic to expect our institutions to achieve is relevant when designing those institutions. If it's not realistic, for example, to assume voters are particularly altruistic or well informed, then we should take this fact into account when designing our political institutions. But the fact that we ought to take such facts into account when designing our institutions does not (absent further argument) entail that the errors the institution will make as a result are permissible or authoritative.

Let us turn now to the worry that the very same non-instrumental value of equality that is alleged to ground democracy's legitimacy and authority might also be threatened—indeed more seriously threatened—by substantively unjust laws. One response is to insist that the type of equality embodied by our democratic procedures is different in kind from the type of equality that can be threatened by substantively unjust laws. Perhaps

---

33. The following point, using this analogy, is made by Wellman in "Space Between," 12.

there is a uniquely "political" or "public" type of equality that is only realized via certain decision-making procedures?[34]

There are two basic problems with this response. First, it's difficult to believe that there is, in fact a uniquely political form of equality that is never threatened by substantively unjust laws. Regardless of whether it is characterized as requiring a form of respect, or a form of public recognition, or as a way by which persons can relate to each other, equality can be imperiled by substantively unjust laws. The only way to resist this conclusion is to make the democratic process itself an essential part of the definition of political or public equality. But doing so threatens to rob democratic egalitarianism of its explanatory power. As Viehoff says, in discussing relational egalitarian theories in particular,

> relational egalitarian accounts do not merely fit existing intuitions about the importance of political equality. They also (and this is the second reason for adopting them) promise to provide independent support for our commitment to this ideal. One of the main challenges in defending procedural egalitarian commitments is to escape the worry that one has simply restated, in slightly different terms, the very democratic intuition one is trying to justify. Relational egalitarian arguments avoid this concern by highlighting these commitments' continuity with other values we care about outside of politics narrowly conceived.[35]

But if the definition of political or public equality makes essential reference to the democratic process itself, it no longer provides independent support for our commitment to these procedures.

Second, even if we set that problem aside, we would still have to show that political or public equality reliably trumps, defeats, or outweighs the importance of averting substantive injustice

---

34. Recall, for example, Christiano's position on the unique status of public equality.

35. Viehoff, "Power and Equality," 4.

across the range of issues where democratic institutions are widely presumed to have authority. Can it really be true that securing the uniquely political form of equality at stake in the democratic process is more important than ensuring people are not unjustly imprisoned for years for conduct that should not be criminalized, or ensuring that people have the legal liberty to marry the person of their choosing, or ensuring that would-be immigrants are not unjustly prevented from immigrating? This strains credulity.

Democratic egalitarians are thus confronted by a dilemma. On the one hand, they can appeal to an independently plausible conception of equality (such as the kind we find, arguably, in certain relationships). As Viehoff notes, doing so promises to provide independent support for the claims made about democracy. But this option comes at a price: any independently plausible conception of equality is virtually certain to be imperiled by many substantively unjust laws, and thus this route leaves the democratic egalitarian vulnerable to the objection that it cannot explain why democratic decisions must—at the bar of equality—take precedence over certain substantive errors. Alternatively, the democratic egalitarian can try to avoid this problem by defining political equality in a way that refers to the democratic process. But this leaves her vulnerable to the charge that, as Viehoff says, the democratic intuition that is supposed to be explained is merely being restated.

Suppose, for the moment, that our democratic egalitarian embraces the first horn of this dilemma—she offers an independently plausibly conception of equality. She might then make the following suggestion: equality of the relevant type requires meeting a certain threshold. So long as inequality is kept within certain limits, the relevant form of egalitarian treatment or relationship is realized. Laws that are only modestly unjust do not exceed the tolerable levels of inequality, and this is why the scope of democratic decision-making can coherently extend to include unjust laws, provided those laws are not gravely or seriously unjust. But laws that are gravely unjust (e.g., laws mandating racial segregation, or laws depriving women of basic political rights) do exceed the tolerable limits of inequality, and this is why democratic majorities lack the authority to enact such laws. This way of conceptualizing the limits of democratic authority and legitimacy may seem to be expressed by Rawls when he writes that "laws cannot be too unjust if they are to be legitimate."[36]

But this view doesn't explain why democratic decisions can be authoritative or legitimate when they are even modestly unjust. If equality (egalitarian relationships or equal respect, etc.) is consistent with some level of substantive injustice, then surely it is also compatible with some modest departures from what an egalitarian political process requires? If we can modestly subvert the democratic process to avert a substantive injustice, this might be consistent with, indeed recommended by, the relevant egalitarian ideal. To avoid this conclusion, our democratic egalitarian would have to insist that while the relevant form of equality is compatible with modest levels of substantive injustice, it is incompatible with even modest deviations from the democratic process. But that, as we have seen, is difficult to believe unless the account of equality has been carefully defined with reference to a process of political decision-making. Opting for such a definition, however, impales us on the second horn of the dilemma.

Conclusion

In chapter 4 we considered instrumental explanations of the authority and legitimacy of political institutions. We saw that the central difficulty with such approaches is the bridging problem: there is no good explanation of how the general instrumental value of an institution necessarily entails the authority or legitimacy of each specific law or directive. Democratic egalitarianism avoids this problem. It insists that there is non-instrumental value in the process of democratic decision-making, and that

36. Rawls, *Political Liberalism*, 428–29.

this non-instrumental value grounds the authority and legitimacy of our democratic laws and policies. But democratic egalitarianism is confronted by a different worry: the weighing problem. Democratic egalitarians must show that the non-instrumental value of equality is so weighty that it justifies the authority or legitimacy of laws even when those laws are substantively unjust. But this is very difficult to do. Some plausible notions of equality might be constitutive of the democratic process, but those very same notions of equality are also clearly threatened by substantively unjust laws. There may be formulations of equality such that the non-instrumental value of equality can only be realized via a decision-making process, and is never threatened by substantively unjust laws, but it's doubtful that such formulations are independently plausible.

None of this is to deny that democratic egalitarianism contains an important element of truth. I share the conviction that there is non-instrumental value realized in an egalitarian process of political decision-making. But this value cannot, on its own, fully explain the scope of democratic authority and legitimacy, and so we must look elsewhere in our search for a solution to the puzzle of legitimate injustice.

6

Sharing Our Mistakes

AS WE'VE SEEN, we can try to explain the phenomenon of legitimate injustice by appealing to either the instrumental or the non-instrumental value of our political institutions. But the views considered so far run into problems. If we appeal purely to the instrumental benefits of political institutions, we face the bridging problem; there's no clear way to connect the general instrumental benefits of our institutions to the legitimacy of specific unjust laws or policies. If, on the other hand, we appeal to some non-instrumental value of democratic institutions, we must surely weigh this value against the disvalue of enforcing particular unjust laws. And thus we face the weighing problem. It seems unlikely that the non-instrumental value of the democratic process is always, or even typically, weightier in the normal range of cases.

Although they face different objections, the theories considered in chapters 4 and 5 do have one feature in common: none of them takes the reality of unjust laws as a starting assumption—as one of the circumstances of politics. This, I think, explains why the different theories all struggle to provide a satisfying explanation of the phenomenon of legitimate injustice. To make progress on the puzzle of legitimate injustice, we should accept that unjust laws are an unavoidable part of our cooperative life. Democratic institutions, even those operating entirely in good faith and doing the best that we can reasonably expect, are not infallible in discerning the substantive content of justice, and thus some amount of unjust legislation is a permanent burden of our cooperative life. Like the other burdens and benefits of that cooperative life, principles of distributive justice must assign rights and duties concerning this burden. I argue that since some unjust laws are an unavoidable burden arising from our shared attempt to live together on fair terms, justice requires that we share in the responsibility for this unavoidable burden. The requirement to share responsibility for our legislative errors offers the best explanation of why, and under what conditions, state officials can permissibly enforce unjust laws and are not liable to being harmed when doing so.[1]

The chapter begins by outlining the sense in which some unjust legislation is an unavoidable burden of our cooperative life and explains why we confront a unique problem with regard to the just allocation of this burden. I consider a familiar proposal, the Perpetrator Pays principle, that might seem apt for addressing the burdens of unjust laws. But this principle, I argue, is not going to be of help in handling the sorts of cases that are our focus. The chapter then addresses skepticism that people's good-faith errors about justice make much difference to what we ought to do or who is liable to harm. I consider Daniel Viehoff's suggestion that state officials are not liable to harm when they enforce unjust laws or policies provided that such officials are, in a specific sense, acting for others. Although Viehoff appeals to distributive fairness, I argue that we have good reasons to resist his proposal. I then provide my own explanation as to why state officials are not liable to harmful interference when enforcing certain unjust laws. I argue that since our democratic efforts to resolve reasonable disagreements will inevitably involve mistakes about justice, it would be unfair and unjust to hold state officials liable for our collective

---

1. Recall, from previous chapters, that to be liable to harmful interference is to forfeit or otherwise lose the moral rights one normally possesses against such harmful interference, whereas to remain nonliable is to retain one's rights against this harmful interference. Even if officials are nonliable, it may still sometimes be permissible to impose harm on such officials, but the justificatory bar for doing is much higher. I return to this point later in the chapter.

mistakes. But what, if anything, explains why state officials act permissibly when enforcing some unjust laws? I argue that state officials will sometimes face choices where all their options are unjust, and thus it must be permissible for them to act unjustly. I also defend the stronger claim that sharing responsibility for our legislative errors entails that state officials can and should permissibly enforce reasonable but unjust democratic laws. The chapter closes first by addressing some objections, and then with some more general reflections on justice and legitimacy.

A Distinctive Burden

Following Rawls, I assume that there will always be reasonable disagreement about what justice permits and requires. For our purposes, we can define reasonable disagreement as disagreement that emerges between sufficiently well-informed, intelligent, and morally conscientious persons who share the view that citizens are free and equal, and that society should be a fair system of social cooperation over time.[2] Although reasonable persons will agree about many things (e.g., that racial discrimination is unjust, that freedom of speech, assembly, and religion are requirements of justice, that people should not be deprived of important opportunities simply on account of their sex or gender), they will disagree about many other political issues, including about how particular principles of justice, such as freedom of speech, ought to be rendered institutionally determinate. I also assume that reasonable disagreements are not necessarily evidence that justice is indeterminate. In at least a range of cases, some of the participants in reasonable disagreements will simply be mistaken about the

---

2. Although I am adopting a broadly Rawlsian account of reasonable disagreement, my view doesn't depend on the details of this account. It depends only on the assumption that disagreement amongst persons (idealized to whatever extent one deems appropriate) about justice is an intractable feature of liberal democratic life.

requirements of justice, and thus they will endorse positions that are reasonable but unjust.

With these assumptions in place, we can anticipate that even in a society where everyone is reasonable in the specified sense, unjust legislation is practically unavoidable. In such a society, citizens won't agree on many important political questions, and there is no effective way to ensure that political power will be exercised only in accordance with the true requirements of justice.[3] If unjust legislation in a cooperative society is unavoidable, even under the very favorable conditions described, then it constitutes a burden of social cooperation that, like other burdens of cooperative political life, must be distributed according to fair principles. Put more simply, we are always going to make democratic mistakes, and a complete account of justice must address this fact.

However, the burdens of unjust law are somewhat distinctive. In standard cases where there is a burden or a benefit to be allocated by distributive principles, there is not much uncertainty or disagreement as to what those burdens and benefits are. Income and wealth are widely understood to be benefits; paying taxes is understood to be a burden. To be sure, there are often disagreements or uncertainty about the precise size of a burden or benefit, or disagreement about the correct way to calculate the amount of harm that someone has suffered. The burdens associated with unjust laws are different, however. They are different because there is widespread and permanent reasonable disagreement about justice. Although we can agree, in the abstract, that our society suffers from the burdens of unjust law, we cannot agree on which laws in particular create those burdens. The durability of this disagreement is a crucial obstacle for any simple proposal regarding how

---

3. As Rawls says, about parties at the stage of the constitutional convention, "even with the best of intentions, their opinions of justice are bound to clash [. . . ;] in adopting some form of majority rule, the parties accept the risks of suffering the defects of one another's knowledge and sense of justice in order to gain the advantages of a legislative procedure." Rawls, *Theory of Justice*, 312.

to allocate or distribute the burdens of unjust law. What should we do about this fact, and what is the fairest way to respond to these burdens?

The Perpetrator Pays

To answer this question, we might appeal to a familiar idea about the fairest way to allocate burdens: a Perpetrator Pays principle. In other domains, such as tort law, when one person treats another unjustly, we aim to shift the burdens of the injustice away from the victim and onto the perpetrator. The perpetrator is required, when possible, to compensate the victim in a way that makes the victim whole. Ideally, the victim should not be left any worse off than she was prior to the rights violation. When we turn our attention to unjust laws, the perpetrators would appear to be the state officials who enforce the laws, perhaps along with the legislators, judges, or executive officials who have enacted the laws or regulations pursuant to which those officials are acting.

But the Perpetrator Pays principle cannot be applied, in any straightforward sense, to the problem of unjust laws. To understand why, we must dig deeper into the Perpetrator Pays principle. When we do so, we can see that there are different possible rationales for the principle.

One rationale is grounded in the importance of correcting wrongs. Suppose A violates B's rights—he damages B's property to the tune of $1000. There is an important sense in which this wrong isn't corrected by B getting $1000 of compensation from some third party, C. This ensures that B is financially no worse off than before, but because A wronged B, correcting A's wrong requires that A be the one who compensates B. A owed B a duty not to damage her property, and since A violated this duty, the remedial duty of compensation is A's and no one else's. If B coincidentally found $1000 on the street on his way to asking A to compensate him, it might make sense for B to say, "I guess no harm done," but it would not make sense for B to say, "I guess no wrong done."

Alternatively, we might ground the Perpetrator Pays principle in an ideal of distributive fairness. Distributive fairness is, on many accounts, responsibility-sensitive. In particular, against a background of equal opportunities, it is fair to hold people substantively responsible for the choice that they make. If A pursues a life of leisure while B toils hard for greater long-run economic security, it seems fair that these choices should, at least in large part, determine their subsequent levels of resources. It wouldn't be fair to take some of B's resources and redistribute them to A since this would make B pay for the costs of A's freely chosen lifestyle. For the same reason, if, in the course of pursuing his own plans, A violates the rights of B, distributive fairness seems to dictate that we shift the costs of this wrongdoing from B back toward A. B should not have to bear the costs that arise from A's pursuit of her own projects.

But neither rationale provides support for the conclusion that the burdens of unjust law should lie primarily with state officials who enforce the laws. State officials who enforce such laws do not commit injustice while pursuing their own private goals. They are instead authorized agents acting on behalf of the political community. Thus, the idea of holding people substantively responsible for the costs of their chosen plans and projects does not support allocating the costs of injustice to state officials. And though state officials do, it seems, wrong others when they enforce unjust law, they do so only as the authorized agents of other principals—the legislature, the courts, and the executive—and those officials also act on behalf of the citizens. If the correction of wrongs requires the perpetrators be held substantively responsible, we cannot focus exclusively on the state officials who enforce unjust legislation.

Skepticism About the Salience of Disagreement

The preceding considerations seem to indicate that we need to widen our focus when asking how to fairly allocate the burdens of unjust laws. These are burdens that arise as a result of conduct undertaken on behalf of the entire political community. Since our laws and institutions are intended to serve the entire political community, when those laws or institutions misfire and create unjust burdens, fairness dictates that those burdens be distributed, if possible, across the political community in accordance with the correct principles of distributive justice. The difficulty lies, however, in determining the practical implications of this general idea. Unlike other issues, where we can all more or less agree what the relevant burdens are, we will not agree which specific laws are unjust, and thus we won't agree on what the burdens are. Without a reasonable consensus about which laws are unjust, there is no straightforward way to distribute the burdens of unjust laws.

A skeptic might take issue with the preceding claim. Of course, people will disagree about the requirements of justice, but the fact of disagreement does not affect the content of the requirements. If the law treats some people unjustly—if their rights are infringed—this is a moral fact to which we ought to respond, and we are obliged to redistribute those burdens in accordance with fair principles. The fact that some people fail to recognize the injustice has no bearing, says the skeptic, on what the real burdens are and who is bearing on them, nor on what we ought to do about them.

But it's not clear what the skeptic is recommending that we do, here and now, in response to the fact that some of our laws are unjust. Perhaps the skeptic is telling us, "Don't pass or enforce unjust laws, and if you have done so, repeal the unjust laws and compensate the victims via public funds." This is good advice for a community where there's no disagreement about requirements of justice, but I can't see how this is helpful for a community with widespread and permanent disagreements about the content of justice. All of us, let's idealistically stipulate, are sincerely aiming to pass only just legislation, but the democratic process frequently yields laws whose status as (un)just is sharply contested. Telling a community, "Don't pass unjust laws, and repeal and compensate if you have done so," is not useful. We already accept this general aim. The problem is that we cannot agree which of the laws are unjust.

At this point our skeptic might say that the recommendation is not addressed to the political community as a whole. It is directed to each individual member of the community. We each face individual decisions, in our roles as citizens or state officials, about whether to comply with unjust legislation, or whether to enforce it. The skeptic, on this interpretation, is telling each person, "There's no duty to comply with unjust laws, and if you're a state official, do not enforce laws that are unjust."[4]

Each of us can try and follow this recommendation. But we must consider the general consequences of doing so. If each of us follows the skeptic's advice, this will not eliminate the reality of some people being subjected to unjust treatment in light of pervasive and permanent disagreement about justice. If each of us decides whether to obey or enforce the law depending on our own judgment as to whether a given law is just or unjust, we will not all make the same decisions. Some state officials will enforce a given law, and others will refuse to enforce it. Some citizens will comply with a given law and others will, when possible, refuse to comply. And if it's common knowledge that everyone is following the skeptic's advice, we might also worry that the rule of law more generally will be difficult to maintain.

This decentralized system is unlikely to be a fair way to address the inevitable burdens of unjust legislation, for several reasons. It makes the enforcement of laws highly unpredictable. Unpredictable law enforcement is bad in a number of ways. It makes effective planning more difficult and costly. It means that like cases will not be treated alike. And it can exacerbate inequalities between rich and poor, for the simple reason that those with fewer resources face greater risks in gambling that laws won't be enforced, whereas those with greater resources are in a better position to gamble on

4. For this general position see, for example, Brennan, *When All Else Fails*; Davis, "Justice: Do It"; Wellman, "Space Between." For a more limited argument in support of the conclusion that consent cannot ground a duty to obey unjust institutions, see van der Vossen, "Consent."

non-enforcement. These are all very substantial costs to the skeptic's decentralizing proposal, and these costs are not offset by important benefits. Individual citizens and officials are not more likely to arrive at correct decisions about justice than democratic institutions.[5] So if we follow the skeptic's recommendation, this will not necessarily reduce the overall amount of injustice.[6] Since the skeptic's proposal creates substantial problems without necessarily reducing the burdens of unjust treatment, we should reject the proposal.

The skeptic might complain that I am misconstruing the proposal. The proposal is not that people ought to refuse to enforce, or refuse to comply with, laws whenever they happen to believe the laws to be unjust. It is that they should do this only when the laws are, in reality, unjust.[7] This proposal would indeed dramatically reduce the overall amount of unjust treatment in our society—so long as most people successfully follow it.

But this reply, though true enough, is not a solution to the practical problem that we face. We don't all agree on the requirements of

5. At least not if we restrict our attention, as I have been doing, to cases of good-faith or reasonable disagreement.

6. Our skeptic might object that this conclusion doesn't follow. The skeptic can be understood only to be encouraging citizens and state officials to refuse to enforce, or comply with, legislation when they believe it to be unjust. The upshot will be that unjust laws will less frequently be enforced than they would be if everyone accepted democratically enacted law as authoritative. But the skeptic is not directing us to unilaterally enforce our own views of justice (when not already reflected by the law). So the proposal is asymmetric. The result will thus be less total enforcement—a shrinking of the power of legal enforcement—and thus the upshot must be less total unjust treatment. But the skeptic's position here depends on a premise that we ought to reject: namely, that injustice only occurs when unjust laws are enforced. This premise is false, since failures to enforce just laws can also result in injustice and rights violations. If the police fail to enforce A's rights against spousal abuse, or decline to enforce B's claim rights to her property, A and B are the victims of injustice. A lot of injustice can arise if we mistakenly refuse to enforce and comply with the requirements of justice.

7. For this kind of response, see Brennan, *When All Else Fails*, 107–15.

justice, and I take this to be a durable fact about any free society. Even in a highly idealized social world—one without bigotry or prejudice, without unreasonable levels of self-interest, and where everyone makes well-informed and good-faith efforts to understand what justice requires—the durable fact of disagreement ensures that we are still confronted by the burdens of injustice. Our practical problem is how to respond to this fact: to figure out the fairest way of addressing this enduring problem. The skeptic's proposal doesn't so much solve the problem as merely idealize it out of existence.

Acting for Others

Let's therefore turn to consider a different, and more promising, approach, one that seeks to explain why state officials are not liable to harm when they enforce (at least some) unjust laws.

Daniel Viehoff argues that state officials are not liable to harm when they act unjustly, if in doing so they are acting for others.[8] To be acting for others, in Viehoff's sense, two conditions must be satisfied:

Deliberative Condition: For Ara to act for Pete on some matter m, (1) Ara's m-related choices must be guided by Pete's interests, and (2) Ara must give the interests of persons other than Pete (including her own) only the deliberative significance that Pete would have reasonably given them in light of his own personal projects and goals.[9]

Justificatory Condition: For Ara to act for Pete on some matter m, it must be the case either (1) that Pete has given his actual consent to Ara's doing so, or (2) that it is in Pete's permissibly pursuable personal interest that Ara act for him even without his actual consent.[10]

---

8. Viehoff, "Legitimate Injustice."
9. Viehoff, "Legitimate Injustice," 332.
10. Viehoff, "Legitimate Injustice," 337.

According to Viehoff, when "these conditions are met, then Ara has effectively lent her agential capacities to Pete, and the costs that arise from her capacities' exercise properly fall on Pete rather than Ara." The explanation for this conclusion appeals to a conception of fairness: "moral norms establish a framework of rights and duties that provides each of us with a fair opportunity to lead her own life—adopt and pursue her personal projects and goals—while respecting others' opportunity to do the same."[11] This picture gives rise to

> a natural answer about how to distribute burdens that arise when an agent fails to abide by the restrictions that protect others. Presumptively, violating these restrictions in the pursuit of one's own projects amounts to unfairly burdening those whom the restrictions protect. So it is only appropriate that they be permitted to redirect (via defensive acts or ex post demands for compensation) most burdens towards the agent whose undisciplined pursuit of her personal projects or goals gives rise to them.[12]

As Viehoff goes on to say, "when something is assigned as a resource to me rather than to you, I rather than you have certain responsibilities for it. If the resource causes undue burdens to others, then I rather than you incur liability."[13]

When Ara acts for Pete in Viehoff's sense, she lends her agency to Pete within some domain. The exercise of Ara's agency is thus best understood as one of Pete's resources. Thus, when Ara errs in exercising this agency and acts unjustly, fairness dictates that it is Pete, and not Ara, who is liable to bear the burdens of Ara's error. This reasoning, Viehoff argues, can be extended to the case of multiple beneficiaries, and this provides the model for state officials

11. Viehoff, "Legitimate Injustice," 324, 325.

12. Viehoff, "Legitimate Injustice," 328.

13. Viehoff, "Legitimate Injustice," 328.

who err. Such officials are not liable to harm if, and because, they act for the sake of those over whom their power is exercised.

Although I share Viehoff's conviction that addressing the problem of unjust laws is a matter of distributive fairness, I am not persuaded that he offers the right account of why state officials are immune from liability when enforcing at least some unjust laws. I begin by highlighting some extensional problems with the account. These extensional problems are illustrative, I argue, of a more fundamental difficulty with Viehoff's proposed rationale.

To begin, the account is too inclusive. For example, on Viehoff's view a government official who is inadvertently negligent while fulfilling her duties, and as a result violates someone's rights, can still satisfy the Deliberative Condition and the Justificatory Condition and thus be nonliable.[14] This conclusion might seem surprising. How can official A negligently threaten harm to some citizen, P, while satisfying the Justificatory Condition's requirement? The answer is that "whether the Justificatory Condition is met must be determined from the ex ante rather than the ex post perspective."[15] Even if A in fact ends up violating P's rights and harming him, it may be true that, ex ante, it was in P's interests for A to act for his sake. That is sufficient, on Viehoff's view, for the Justificatory Condition to be satisfied.

But I think this leads to unacceptable results. Ex ante, it may be in citizen Pete's interests for police officer Ara to patrol his neighborhood. But if Ara negligently ignores key information and shoots at Pete, mistakenly believing him to be a dangerous suspect, I think it's clear that Ara is liable to defensive harm. And the account will be over-inclusive in other ways, too. State officials who are bigoted or prejudiced and who violate the rights of citizens due to their bigotry or prejudice might still satisfy the Justificatory Condition and the

14. Viehoff accepts this implication of his account: "Legitimate Injustice." 306, 344–45
15. Viehoff, "Legitimate Injustice," 340.

Deliberative Condition, but I don't think such officials are immune from necessary and proportionate harm if they commit injustice as a result of that bigotry or prejudice.

Moreover, as well as being in various ways too inclusive, the account is, in several respects, not inclusive enough. I don't believe, for example, that the Deliberative Condition needs to be satisfied in order for an agent to be nonliable.[16] Suppose I am confronted by a wrongful aggressor who is intent on killing me. The aggressor is also intent on killing you, though I'm unaware of this fact. I use necessary and proportionate force against the aggressor, but in doing so I will inadvertently, and non-negligently break your legs. I do not satisfy the Deliberative Condition (I am not guided by your interests but rather my own), but I think it's clear that I am not liable to defensive harm to protect your legs. I have, after all, saved your life, and the harm that I threaten to impose is non-negligent.

These problems of extension highlight problems with the conception of distributive fairness to which Viehoff appeals. Fairness sometimes requires that we bear the costs of our mistakes. As Viehoff emphasizes, this is most likely to be the case when we are using our fair share of resources to pursue our personal plans or projects. It doesn't seem fair for others to pay for the costs associated with our pursuit of our private projects. Viehoff argues that this rationale extends to cases where A lends her agency to P. A's mistakes are assimilated to P—it's as if P makes the mistakes himself using his own resources. But there are problems with this suggestion.

First, if A acts to advance P's permissibly pursuable interests, this is not the same thing as P pursuing his own plans and projects. What is in P's interests might depart from P's plans

---

16. This is not, strictly speaking, in conflict with anything that Viehoff says, since he is offering sufficient, rather than necessary, conditions for nonliability. Still, I think it's indicative that the account is perhaps not pointing us in exactly the right direction.

and projects. P might have a plan to pursue a disastrous career as a cat trainer, and A might best promote P's interests by thwarting this plan and directing P toward a career to which he is more suited. If A does this, then this isn't a case of P pursuing his plans and projects. A's paternalistic action to benefit P is more plausibly construed as one of A's projects, and so costs arising from mistakes with this project more plausibly attach to A.

Second, and relatedly, when state officials enforce laws, they are typically not best understood as helping those subject to the laws advance their own personal plans and projects. They are better understood as playing a role in a wider system that adjudicates in conflicts between citizens, specifies what rights and duties citizens possess, and enforces claims of justice. In performing these roles, state officials are not helping people pursue their private projects, except very indirectly. They are rather helping to create and maintain a fair system of rules within which each person is then at liberty to pursue their plans and projects. It thus does not seem apt to suggest that the costly mistakes that officials make, when acting in this capacity, are relevantly analogous to the costly mistakes an individual person makes in pursuing her conception of the good. When I pursue my interest in baseball, I should have to pay for the costs if my ball breaks your window. But if a state official mistakenly assigns a property right to you when that property ought rightfully to be mine, this official is not helping either of us pursue our projects; rather, she is regulating what each of us may permissibly use in the pursuit of our projects.

The burden of unjust law is not a by-product of some individuals pursuing their private conceptions of the good. We thus cannot appeal to what fairness requires in terms of holding individuals substantively responsible for the costs that arise when they pursue their own conceptions of the good. Instead, we should recognize the problem of unjust law as a shared or common burden that arises as a result of our good-faith efforts to determine what justice permits and requires.

Disagreeing and Sharing Our Mistakes

Sometimes, perhaps quite often, we make mistakes about the requirements of justice. They are mistakes because, although we make a sincere and good-faith effort to determine what justice requires, we fail to arrive at the correct view. As a result, we pass legislation that is unjust. Such mistakes are a more or less permanent feature of any pluralistic, democratic society. What is the fairest way to tackle this problem?

The following analogy might be helpful. Consider an academic department such as a philosophy department where the faculty aim to be self-governing in an egalitarian way. The members sharply disagree about subject matter and methodology—about how good teaching and research ought to be done. Many of these disagreements have right and wrong, or at least better and worse, answers: some members are mistaken on some of these issues, though of course there's no agreement about who the mistaken ones may be. Notwithstanding these disagreements, the department has lots of decisions to make: which courses to teach, which graduate students to admit, which new faculty to hire, and so on. Given their disagreements, all the members anticipate that it's certain that some of the decisions they will make will be incorrect, and that there won't be agreement about which decisions are the mistakes. What's a fair way for the faculty to manage this problem?

Suppose that the faculty makes important decisions via a democratic vote, but when those votes are substantively mistaken the office-holder who carries out or enforces the decision (such as the director of undergraduate studies when the decision pertains to undergraduate teaching) is uniquely responsible for the mistake. This is manifestly unfair to the office-holder, since the mistake in question is not uniquely hers—it is rather the collective mistake of the faculty and thus the faculty members should collectively share responsibility for their mistake.

I claim that something analogous is true in political life when we focus on reasonable disagreements. We cannot eliminate the reality of unjust legislation, but we can at least aim to ensure that all members of the political community share equally in the responsibility for the imposition of unjust laws via a democratic process, rather than outsourcing this responsibility to state officials. There are at least two dimensions to sharing responsibility for our mistakes in this way.

First, a state official does not have the discretion to subvert, or act contrary to, democratically authorized directives when those directives fall within the scope of reasonable disagreement. On the alternative view—whereby state officials have the leeway to disregard reasonable democratic law that they sincerely believe to be unjust—officials would effectively be in the position of always bearing greater responsibility for imposing unjust laws or policies, since they would not simply be the authorized agents of a democratic community, but would also be required to make their own reasonable determination regarding the (in)justice of any law or policy when deciding how to act.[17] We can return to the analogy of an academic department. Suppose faculty vote on all major decisions connected to undergraduate teaching, but ultimately the director of undergraduate studies must always consult her own judgment and may permissibly ignore the faculty's vote whenever she sincerely believes it to be mistaken. In this department, the responsibility of imposing mistaken decisions on undergraduates is not shared equally: the director of undergraduate studies bears a much larger share of this responsibility than anyone else.

Second, and relatedly, state officials who implement democratically authorized directives when those directives fall within the scope of reasonable disagreement are not specially liable to harm. When the laws or directives these officials enforce are unjust, the error is not theirs, but rather one that we collectively make. To hold state officials uniquely or specially liable would be deeply unfair—it would be to hold state officials substantively

17. Of course sometimes officials will be given considerable discretion regarding how to act, but that discretion must itself be something that is ultimately authorized by our democratic institutions.

responsible for an unavoidable shared or collective burden of our cooperative political life.[18]

In sum, on my view, a state official is nonliable to defensive harm when they enforce an unjust law and

a) the official is non-negligently acting within the scope of her authority in the service of
b) enforcing or otherwise carrying out democratically authorized law or policy that
c) constitutes the resolution of a reasonable disagreement.

Although also grounded in a view about distributive fairness, this proposal contrasts with Viehoff's in several significant respects. First, state officials are not immune to harm when they act negligently. My account thus has no difficulty in explaining why the police officer who negligently threatens to harm a citizen is liable to harm. My account will also not grant immunity to state

18. One might protest that even if it's unfair to hold state officials uniquely or specially liable to defensive harm, they still share in the responsibility for the error like every other citizen, and thus it does not follow that state officials are nonliable to defensive harm. Whether they are liable depends on whether one can be liable to defensive harm for the unjust conduct of a large collective when one shares equally in the responsibility for that conduct with millions of others. Perhaps even when someone is only one amongst millions who share responsibility for an unjust action, that person can be fully or partially liable to defensive harm, since that person at least shares in the responsibility. Jeff McMahan, for example, has argued that even a slight difference in moral responsibility for an unjust threat can justify making the more responsible party liable to the entirety of the unjust harm when the harm is not divisible. See McMahan, "Basis of Moral Liability," 394–95. A full assessment of this proposal requires delving into the details of the necessary and sufficient conditions for liability to defensive harm, something that is beyond the scope of this chapter, though I have expressed my views about this elsewhere: see Quong, *Morality of Defensive Force*, ch. 2. Here I simply note that even on McMahan's account, there must be some difference in the degree of moral responsibility between parties A and V to hold A liable to defensive harm. But if we collectively share in the responsibility for reasonable but unjust laws, there will be no such difference in responsibility between a state official and any other member of the polity, and thus no basis for singling out the state official as liable. This conclusion does depend, however, on some further assumptions about moral responsibility that I lack the space to defend here.

officials who are guided by bigotry or prejudice (*ex hypothesi* such aims are not matters of reasonable disagreement).

Second, the account deems state officials nonliable even when they are not guided by the interests of those over whom they exercise power, provided they satisfy (a)–(c) above. Consider a state official who is guided by the aim of impressing her superiors—she isn't guided by the institution's purposes or the interests of those over whom she exercises power. If her superiors directed her to take illegal or undemocratic action, she would do so without hesitation. But as it happens her superiors don't do this—she is directed only to enforce democratically authorized legislation that falls within the boundaries of reasonable disagreement. I don't think this state official is liable to harm when she does her job and enforces an unjust law. The counterfactual choices that she would make if she had different superiors are irrelevant to her liability.

Third, on this account it need not be the case that the interests of those non-consensually subjected to the power of state officials are ex ante best served by those officials taking up their roles. Suppose a newly constituted, liberal democratic country (emerging after decolonization) holds its first democratic elections. One party wins a legislative majority and passes various laws, all of which are reasonable, but some of these laws are mistakes and result in substantial injustices. Suppose it's a predictable feature of newly decolonized governments that they commit more injustices than more established liberal democratic regimes, and thus it is predictable that had the original (liberal democratic) colonial power continued to rule, the population would have been subjected to fewer, or less serious, injustices. On Viehoff's view, the new domestic government's officials do not satisfy the Justificatory Condition (because it's predictable that they won't perform as well as the previous colonial regime), and thus might be liable to harm. My account doesn't have this implication.

These extensional differences between our accounts are explained by a deeper difference regarding how we conceptualize fairness as bearing on the problem of unjust legislation. Viehoff, as we have seen, appeals to a view about the fair allocation of costs between private parties pursuing their own good:

> a natural answer about how to distribute burdens that arise when an agent fails to abide by the restrictions that protect others. Presumptively, violating these restrictions in the pursuit of one's own projects amounts to unfairly burdening those whom the restrictions protect. So it is only appropriate that they be permitted to redirect (via defensive acts or ex post demands for compensation) most burdens towards the agent whose undisciplined pursuit of her personal projects or goals gives rise to them.[19]

On my view, by contrast, the relevant burdens of unjust law do not arise as a result of people pursuing their own good with their own resources. They arise, rather, as a result of our collective and reasonable efforts to determine what justice requires. The burdens are to be shared because they are an unavoidable by-product of our collective attempt to live with one another on fair terms. This is a collective project we are obligated to undertake. When state officials make nonnegligent mistakes as a result of this collective effort, they are mistakes to be shared by all those who are duty-bound to participate in the collective effort, and this explains why such officials are nonliable.[20] But not all the mistakes state officials make are part of this collective effort, and so not all their mistakes should be shared.

Permissible Injustice

I have argued that state officials are not liable to harmful interference when they enforce reasonable but unjust laws and policies that arise from the democratic process. But legitimacy, as we have been using the term, implies not merely that state officials are immune from liability, but also that those officials act permissibly when they enforce laws or policies. In this section and the next, I argue that state

19. Viehoff, "Legitimate Injustice," 328.

20. For an alternative view, one that insists it is sometimes fair to hold state officials liable in such conditions, see Pasternak, No Justice, chs. 4 and 5.

officials can also act permissibly when they enforce reasonable but unjust laws that emerge from the democratic process.

The first step in the argument is to establish that it can sometimes be—indeed must be—permissible for state officials to act unjustly.[21] We have been assuming that there will be a great deal of reasonable disagreement about justice, including in response to difficult questions such as "What rates of income tax are required as a matter of justice?" or "Should freedom of expression extend to protect those who deny the Holocaust to promote anti-Semitism?" But the fact that people will reasonably disagree about the requirements of justice doesn't imply that there are no correct answers to these questions, or that the answers are indeterminate.

Along with many democratic theorists, I believe that people have a claim of justice to an equal (and positive) say in resolving reasonable disagreements about justice. To disregard democratic decisions whenever one thinks they are unjust is a refusal to participate on equal terms in the political process with other reasonable people. To be clear, I'm not suggesting that unreasonable views about justice—those that are, in some sense, beyond the pale, such as the violations of core liberal rights and freedoms— should be implemented if selected by a democratic process. I'm only suggesting that there is a claim of justice to have an egalitarian democratic process for resolving reasonable disagreements.

Suppose, for the sake of argument, that the correct account of justice includes a very expansive principle of free speech: one that provides a protected claim right against interference to people who engage in hate speech, such as Nazis who wish to march and chant anti-Semitic slurs in Jewish neighborhoods. But the issue is one over which reasonable people disagree, and after a fair democratic process, our political community enacts a law that prohibits certain forms of hate speech, including the Nazis' anti-Semitic march.

If state officials fail to do what they have been directed to do by a fair democratic process, the government will be acting

---

21. The material in the remainder of this section reproduces and revises some material from Quong, "Legitimate Injustice," 227–31.

unjustly—failing to respect what justice requires regarding the resolution of reasonable political disputes. However, if state officials enforce the democratically enacted law prohibiting the march, they act contrary to the principle of free speech, another requirement of justice. So state officials will act unjustly whatever they do. If we assume that at least one option from an agent's feasible set must be permissible, then it must be possible for the state's officials to act permissibly and yet unjustly.

Here is the argument stated a bit more precisely:[22]

P1. Reasonable disagreement about justice is possible, even when there are determinate answers about what justice requires.

P2. Justice requires giving people equal opportunity to exercise political power in cases of reasonable disagreement.

22. There are two further issues worth noting about the argument. First, democracy (at least in its standard form) is not the only way to grant people an equal opportunity to exercise political power in cases of reasonable disagreement; sortition or lottocracy—where legislative officials are chosen at random—would also seem to achieve this objective. I think that in a wide range of circumstances there are compelling reasons to prefer democratic voting over sortition, but making this case is beyond the scope of this chapter. The success of the argument above, however, does not depend on voting being preferable to sortition; we could replace the words "democratic process" with "lottocracy" in premises 3 and 5 and the substance of the argument would not be affected. Second, some might worry the argument is vulnerable to something close to self-defeat, because one of the issues over which there can be reasonable disagreement is the principle expressed in P2. For example, Jason Brennan argues that there is a right to a competent electorate, and this right conflicts with existing forms of democracy that do not condition the right to vote on being competent. If Brennan's position is at least a reasonable one, then the argument apparently entails that democracy itself must be subject to an egalitarian decision process, a process which could presumably yield a result whereby democratic institutions are rejected. Again, a full response to this worry is beyond the scope of this chapter, but I'll make one brief point. The argument presented here can easily be revised to incorporate a competency requirement. Suppose the right to an equal opportunity to exercise political power is restricted to those who satisfy the competency requirement. That narrower constituency might still err and enact substantively unjust legislation, at which point we still get the dilemma described in C1. For Brennan's position, see Brennan, "Right to a Competent Electorate."

P3. If the state fails to enact and pursue a reasonable position that emerges from a fair democratic process, it violates the requirement in P2, and so acts unjustly.

P4. At least one option from an agent's feasible set must be morally permissible.

P5. A fair democratic process sometimes results in the selection of a policy that is reasonable but substantively unjust.

Therefore,

C1. it must be permissible for the state to act unjustly, either by violating the principle requiring equal opportunity to exercise political power, or else by imposing a substantively unjust policy.

Each premise of this argument is difficult to reject. Denying P1 is implausible. It's not credible to suppose that all our disagreements about justice are driven by self-interest, prejudice, or irrationality. I also do not think it is plausible to suppose, as we have seen some Kantians do, that almost all substantive issues of social or distributive justice are largely indeterminate. Many specific questions about the requirements of justice may be indeterminate, but this fact is consistent with P1. P1 makes only the very modest claim that reasonable disagreement is possible, even when there are determinate answers about the requirements of justice.

Denying P2 seems almost as difficult, though Kit Wellman has recently made claims that might constitute a rejection of P2. He says,

> I worry, though, that it depends on a misunderstanding of the moral value of procedural justice. In my view, justice in both its procedural and substantive incarnations provides side-constraints to be respected, rather than competing values to be promoted [...;] even if an egalitarian democrat's argument establishes that each of us has a right to democratic governance, it at most establishes that acting justly includes an additional side-constraint, but this is very different from showing that

procedural justice is a value which sometimes outweighs, over-rides, or undercuts the moral imperative to respect nonproce-dural rights.[23]

In this passage Wellman points out something that, as we have seen, democratic egalitarians sometimes ignore: the mere fact that there is something valuable about democratic procedures does not suf-fice, on its own, to show that the scope of the right to democratic governance extends to cover substantively unjust decisions.

But the idea that claims of justice operate as side-constraints is notoriously tricky. Most obviously, what happens when two claims of justice conflict? Some proponents of the side-constraint view argue that this is conceptually impossible. Claims of justice, by their very nature, can never come into conflict.[24] But this very dif-ficult to accept, and is sharply at odds with commonsense morality. This view requires either that the content of justice be extremely sparse, so as to eliminate the possibility of conflicts arising, or else a kind of specificationism about justice, such that whenever we have an apparent conflict of claims we must conclude that, in those specific circumstances, only one of the claims turns out to be a valid claim of justice. I think there are compelling reasons to reject both of these options, though it would be too much of a digression to lay these out here.

If we accept the commonsense view that claims of justice can sometimes conflict, then we can easily accept P2. And it's worth emphasizing how revisionary and counterintuitive it would be to deny P2. To deny P2 would mean that there need be nothing unjust about stuffing ballot boxes or suppressing other people's votes, provided doing so was a way of ensuring that only truly just policies are enacted.

P3 seems uncontroversial if P2 has been accepted. P4 is not uncontroversial: a minority of philosophers claim that in some

23. Wellman, "Space Between," pp. 6–7. For remarks similar to Wellman's, see Øverland and Barry, "Do Democratic Societies Have a Right."
24. For a defense of this view, see Steiner, *Essay on Rights*, 86–101.

situations an agent will act wrongly regardless of what she does. Entering this debate is beyond the scope of this chapter, so I'll simply say that, along with many others, I think P4 is true: there must be a permissible option in an agent's set of choices.[25] And P5 does not seem controversial if P1 is accepted.

In sum, when the democratic process produces a reasonable but unjust law, state officials are thus faced with two main options (subvert the democratic law, or enforce it), both of which involve injustice. If some option from an agent's set must be permissible, then it must be permissible for state officials to act unjustly in these circumstances.

Which Injustice?

The preceding argument only establishes that state officials can permissibly commit injustice when they confront cases where the democratic process yields a reasonable but unjust law. The argument above is silent, however, regarding which injustice state officials ought to commit. Perhaps, as Stemplowska and Swift have suggested, there is no general answer to this question, and instead the decision can only be made on a case-by-case basis by weighing the relevant reasons in each instance?[26] In this section I argue for a different conclusion: namely, that in cases of reasonable but unjust law state officials typically should enforce the unjust law rather than ignore or subvert it.

To establish this conclusion, we need to return to the idea of sharing responsibility for our (reasonable) legislative errors. I suggested earlier that to share responsibility for our mistakes, state officials cannot have the leeway to disregard the results of the democratic process when they believe (even correctly) that the result of the process is a reasonable but unjust law. If officials are permitted to exercise discretion about the imposition of

---

25. For an overview of this debate, see McConnell, "Moral Dilemmas."
26. Stemplowska and Swift, "Dethroning Democratic Legitimacy."

reasonable democratically authorized laws and policies, then we would no longer be sharing equally and collectively in the responsibility for our errors. Officials would be in the effective position of always bearing greater responsibility, since they would be required to make their own determination regarding the (in)justice of any law when deciding how to act.

We can make this suggestion more precise. Taking collective or shared responsibility for our reasonable legislative errors requires state officials to ignore or set aside certain facts as potential reasons for action when deliberating about what to do. In particular, the fact [the law is unjust] must be excluded from state officials' reasoning. State officials should inquire whether the law or policy was promulgated via the appropriate process, and they should inquire as to whether the law or policy falls within the domain of the reasonable. But if the answer to those questions is "yes," state officials are precluded from engaging in first-order reasoning about whether the law or policy is (un)just. In this way, state officials are not responsible for deciding whether a law or policy is just—they are merely the authorized agents of the political community, enacting the outcome of our collective effort to resolve reasonable disagreements about politics.

Because the fact [the law is unjust] is excluded from the deliberations of state officials, when laws are reasonable but unjust, state officials will thus typically be obligated to enforce such laws, since the reason that is most likely to tell against enforcement is excluded from their deliberations.[27]

The scope of this argument is limited in at least two plausible ways. First, the argument only covers unjust legislation that arises from reasonable disagreements. It doesn't extend to unjust legislation over which there can be no reasonable disagreement: for

27. I say "typically" because there will be cases where state officials have other reasons—unconnected to the injustice of the law—that count against enforcement of the law, and these reasons may be sufficient to countenance unjustly subverting the democratic process.

example, proposed legislation that would permit religious persecution or racial discrimination. This coheres, I suspect, with many people's attitudes regarding the legitimate authority of the state. We have to put up with some unjust legislation, but there are limits—laws that clearly conflict with fundamental liberal egalitarian principles cannot be legitimate, regardless of their procedural pedigree.

Second, the argument does not apply (or at least not in the same way) in cases where a political community's institutions are systematically failing to allocate fairly the burdens and benefits of cooperative life. Consider a society with a pattern of racial injustice and discrimination, and where the burdens of injustice disproportionately fall on members of a particular racial minority. Since the burdens and benefits of cooperative life are already not being shared fairly, it's no longer plausible to suppose that granting state officials the permission to enforce reasonable but unjust legislation that has emerged from the democratic process is a constitutive part of sharing fairly in the burdens of cooperative life. Indeed, in cases such as this it's not even clear that the members of the unjustly oppressed group have duties to refrain from interfering with most legislation regardless of whether its content is unjust. Refraining may be burdensome, and the members of this group are already not being accorded a fair share of society's benefits.[28] The same conclusion would apply to a political community where wealth and political power are distributed so unequally that members from the poorest socio-economic groups bear a significantly disproportionate share of the burdens, while the rich are largely able to shield themselves from most burdens of cooperative life. The argument thus only applies under reasonably favorable conditions where the burdens and benefits are not being systematically distributed in a clearly unjust way.[29]

28. In this way the argument is congruent with the position developed in Shelby, *Dark Ghettos*, chs. 7 and 8.

29. In this respect I follow Rawls, who says, regarding the obligation to obey unjust laws, that "the parties agree to put up with unjust laws only on certain

To some this limitation of the argument's scope might seem a weakness—it might seem to entail that the argument doesn't apply to contemporary liberal democracies such as the United States. In my view, however, it is a strength. People who live in grossly unjustly deprived communities in the United States are not being granted a fair opportunity to share in the burdens and benefits of cooperative life, and so I find it plausible to be skeptical that state officials can permissibly impose further injustices on such communities, even if the laws being imposed have the appropriate procedural pedigree.[30]

Objections

In this section I outline and reply to four potential objections.

The Costs of Unjust Law Are More Important

Some might wonder whether my focus on the permissibility of enforcement of unjust laws and officials' associated nonliability is of much consequence. Surely, says the critic, the most important issue when it comes to sharing our mistakes is that there be a fair distribution of the costs of those mistakes. Those who are subjected to the harms or costs of unjust law ought to be compensated by those more fortunate members of the political community who have not had to suffer these harms or costs. For example, when we

---

conditions. Roughly speaking, in the long run the burden of injustice should be more or less evenly distributed over different groups in society [...]. Therefore the duty to comply is problematic for permanent minorities that have suffered from injustice for many years." Rawls, *Theory of Justice*, 312.

30. Note that the claim here is about whether state officials act permissibly in imposing unjust laws on members of grossly unjustly deprived communities. Even if we conclude that they do not, it does not necessarily follow that it is permissible to use defensive violence against such officials. Whether such violence is permissible depends on various circumstantial details concerning the proportionality and necessity of such acts of defensive violence.

discover that someone has been mistakenly imprisoned for a crime that they did not commit, that person is entitled to compensation drawn from public funds.

The problem with this suggestion, however, is one to which I've already alluded. The fact of reasonable disagreement is assumed to be permanent. We will thus never agree on which (reasonable) laws are unjust. The case of unjust law is thus not analogous to a case where we discover someone has been unjustly convicted of a crime. In the latter, but not the former, case there's an objective and widely accepted standard for assessing the correctness of a conviction. The special problem we face with unjust law is the general awareness that some of our laws are indeed unjust, combined with the permanent disagreement concerning which laws these are. The proposal to simply compensate those who have been the victims of unjust laws is thus practically hopeless—we might as well assume away the problem of unjust law altogether.

There are, however, institutional steps we might take to try to spread the risks of suffering unjust law more equitably. For example, laws over which there is reasonable disagreement should not be constitutionally enshrined or made too difficult to overturn, since doing so risks forcing some people to suffer permanently the burdens of unjust law without the chance of reprieve. Other things being equal, we also have reasons to prefer decentralized forms of political decision-making with regard to many issues over which there is reasonable disagreement.[31] This can allow different jurisdictions to adopt different policies, thus potentially mitigating the number of people who will be forced to live under laws that they find to be deeply unjust. To be sure, a subjective belief that a law is unjust does not entail that the law is in fact unjust. But it's also true that one of the burdens of unjust law is the alienation those subject to the law may experience.

Fairness in addressing the burden of unjust law also speaks against unilateral disobedience and defiance whenever one believes

31. For a proposal along these lines, see King, "Federal Structure."

laws to be unjust. Not everyone has the same opportunities to disobey or defy laws that they believe to be unjust. In particular, those with wealth and other social advantages are more likely to be able to engage in disobedience without suffering adverse consequences. The preceding might sound objectionably like leveling down: the fortunate should be made to suffer the burden of unjust law, since the less fortunate are less able to engage in successful defiance. But it's not obvious that what will in fact occur amounts to leveling down. When those with the means to do so defy laws that they believe to be unjust, they may be correct that the law in question is unjust, but they may also be mistaken. Given our assumptions, there's no reason to believe that widespread compliance is more likely to be a net loss at the bar of justice as compared to a world with widespread noncompliance.

The Need for Balance

Suppose we grant that it would be, in one way, unfair to hold state officials liable for our collective legislative errors. Nevertheless, says a critic, we must balance this unfairness against the substantive injustice that might be suffered by those upon whom unjust laws are enforced. Any sensible approach to balancing these considerations, continues the critic, will frequently yield the conclusion that the burdens of those facing substantive injustice are much weightier than any unfairness in holding state officials liable to harm. Consider, for example, citizens who are unjustly deprived of adequate access to health care, or citizens who are unjustly imprisoned for years for possession of recreational drugs. These citizens suffer grave forms of injustice and harm that can surely be weightier than the interest in ensuring that state officials are not unfairly held liable to harm for enforcing such unjust laws. This might appear to undermine my view whereby state officials are never liable to harm provided they are non-negligently enforcing democratically authorized laws that are matters of reasonable dispute. Instead, the critic argues, we must balance the different considerations on a case-by-case basis. Sometimes the importance of averting substantive injustice will be weighty enough to deem state officials liable, even though doing so is unfair to those officials.

We should reject this suggestion, though we needn't entirely reject the idea of balancing. The critic errs in supposing that the liability of state officials is determined by balancing the substantive injustice of particular laws against the unfairness of holding state officials liable to harm for enforcing democratically authorized legislation. Liability to defensive harm is not determined in this way. Suppose a lethal projectile is headed toward five innocent victims. The victims have two ways to save their lives: (a) redirect the projectile to the left where it will kill innocent bystander Albert, or (b) redirect the projectile to the right where it will paralyze innocent bystander Betty. It is not fair for Albert to be killed, nor is it fair for Betty to suffer paralysis, but plausibly it is less unfair for Betty to suffer paralysis. It does not follow from the fact that it is less unfair for Betty to suffer paralysis, however, that she is liable to suffer this harm—that she has lost her claim against the imposition of this harm. The five innocent victims have a lesser-evil justification for redirecting the projectile toward Betty, but if they do so, they infringe a right of Betty's, because she is not liable.

We should take a similar approach to the permissibility of resisting state officials who act non-negligently in enforcing reasonable but unjust laws. State officials are not liable to harm in such cases, but it does not follow that it is never morally permissible to resist the imposition of such laws by interfering with their actions. But since there is no liability justification for engaging in these forms of resistance, such resistance would have to be justified in terms of lesser evil. Lesser-evil justifications concern cases where it is justifiable to impose harm on persons who are not liable to suffer that harm to avert some much more serious injustice or consequence befalling another group of people. Notably, lesser-evil justifications are not simple consequentialist justifications: it's not permissible to harm nonliable people whenever there is some marginal gain to be had by doing so. Lesser-evil justifications require the benefits of acting to be *widely proportionate*. Wide proportionality, unlike a simple consequentialist calculation, requires the benefits of acting to be much greater than the harms caused. Classic discussions in the literature suggest that foreseeably harming a nonliable person (non-intentionally and not as a means) might only be widely proportionate when doing so is needed to avert at least five times as many equivalent harms. The wide proportionality ratio of benefits to harms in cases where the nonliable person is harmed intentionally, or as a means, is generally believed to be far greater, though there's no consensus on what exactly the ratio is in such cases.

This suggests a different, and more plausible, picture of the permissibility of violently resisting reasonable but unjust law than the one proposed by the critic above. The use of violence against state officials who act non-negligently in enforcing reasonable but unjust laws cannot be permissible unless it is widely proportionate. But it's difficult to satisfy the condition of wide proportionality, particularly when the harms imposed on state officials are deliberate, or serve as a means to an end. Cases of permissible violent resistance against reasonable but unjust laws are thus likely to be relatively rare (excluding conditions of systemic injustice of the sort discussed earlier). This conclusion seems plausible. Laws concerning the distribution of income and wealth, or educational opportunities, or health care might be substantively unjust, but so long as the laws are subject to reasonable disagreement, violent resistance against state officials seems unlikely to be permissible precisely because such resistance seems unlikely to be proportionate.[32] Things are different when the laws are not merely

---

32. I think Pasternak would disagree, in part because she holds that state officials, particularly police officers, can be liable to harm under these conditions. See Pasternak, *No Justice*, chs. 4 and 5.

unjust, but also fall outside the scope of reasonable disagreement. Laws grounded in bigotry or racial prejudice, for example, are outside the scope of reasonable disagreement, and thus state officials enforcing such laws may be liable to defensive harm. This explains why it's much easier to justify violent resistance to such laws; imposing harm on those liable to suffer it is much easier to justify than imposing harm on the nonliable.

Why Reasonable Disagreement?

I have suggested that a certain sub-set of unjust laws—those arising from our reasonable disagreements—should be treated as an unavoidable burden of our cooperative life, and something for which we must collectively share responsibility. This focus on reasonable disagreement is vulnerable to skepticism from at least two directions.

On the one hand, some doubt that disagreement, however reasonable, can be relevant to the determination of our rights and duties or the deontic status of our acts. Here is Kit Wellman expressing a version of this worry:

> if the sincere but unreasonable beliefs of the majority do not change the moral status of a given course of action, why think that the beliefs of the majority have this moral power as long as the beliefs are not unreasonable? It strikes me as more natural to conclude that the majority has made a reasonable mistake than to suppose that the majority's not unreasonable judgment changes the moral status of a course of action.[33]

But even if one agrees with Wellman that the reasonable beliefs of the majority cannot change the deontic status of an act—it cannot, for example, render an act permissible that would otherwise be impermissible—it can still be true that the reasonable beliefs of a majority change our rights and duties with regard to one another.

33. Wellman, "Space Between," 18.

Even if state officials act impermissibly in enforcing unjust laws, they can still have protected claim rights in doing so. There's nothing incoherent about having a claim right that protects one from harm while being engaged in wrongful conduct, and indeed a right to do wrong in this sense is familiar from ordinary interpersonal morality. Moreover, as I argued previously, the reasonable but mistaken beliefs of a majority can change the deontic status of an act provided it's true that there is a claim of justice to participate on equal terms in the political decision-making of one's community, and the scope of that right is not restricted to those who never err about justice. If we assume at least one option from an agent's set must be permissible, then the reasonable mistakes of the majority do have the capacity to change the deontic status of state officials' acts.

Others might think that the focus on unjust laws over which there can be reasonable disagreement is too narrow. For example, many existing political disagreements in the United States are not best characterized as reasonable disagreements. But, says this skeptic, if those views nevertheless win the day in a free and fair democratic process, then state officials who enforce the resulting legislation should still be nonliable; they are, after all, still merely acting as the authorized agents of the wider political community. State officials should only be liable to harm if they act unjustly in ways that go beyond their mandate.

But the mere fact of being authorized or directed by others is clearly insufficient to render one immune from liability. Hit men act as the authorized agents of others, but this does not absolve them of liability. This example might seem unfair—hit men do something that is clearly illegal, whereas state officials who enforce the law do not. But there's nothing magical about the law that should absolve people from liability to harm. Officials enforcing racial segregation were frequently acting within the law, but I think they were potentially liable to defensive harm.[34]

34. This doesn't entail that state officials may never be partially or even fully excused for their actions for reasons of ignorance or duress. Whether some degree of

The skeptic might amend her proposal to require that state officials also act in ways that are consistent with basic human rights and other rights as set out in a constitution to be nonliable. But once the proposal is specified in this way, it no longer serves as a clear alternative to the focus on reasonable disagreement; it rather constitutes a particular way of specifying the boundaries of the reasonable. I think the boundaries of the reasonable should be drawn more narrowly, but however the notion is specified, it plays a crucial role in demarcating the range of laws or policies within which state officials are immune from liability. Some policies are beyond the pale, and we need not treat such policies as unavoidable costs of living cooperatively together. But over some range, we must accept good-faith disagreement as permanent feature of our cooperative life, and thus errors within that range must be conceptualized as shared or collective burdens.

The Freedom and Power of State Officials

Consider one final objection. Some might insist that our unjust laws are not a burden to be collectively shared, for two reasons. First, ordinary citizens exercise virtually no causal control over the democratic process, nor do they have any causal control over the vast range of issues with regard to which state officials exercise considerable discretion. Second, in liberal societies, state officials are not conscripts: they are paid employees who make the voluntary choice to take up a role. These two facts in combination, says the critic, imply that unjust laws are not the sort of thing for which we must share responsibility. The responsibility lies entirely, or least largely, with the elected officials who pass the unjust laws, and the state officials who enforce such legislation.

---

culpability is a necessary condition for liability to defensive harm is an issue beyond the scope of the current chapter, though I have expressed my views on this issue in Quong, *Morality of Defensive Force*, ch. 2.

In reply, I think it's useful to distinguish three questions regarding reasonable but unjust laws: (a) are ordinary citizens substantively liable to bear costs to compensate the victims of unjust laws; (b) are ordinary citizens blameworthy for unjust laws; and (c) are state officials liable to harm for enforcing unjust laws?[35]

There are, of course, competing theories of the necessary and sufficient conditions to be liable to bear compensatory duties, and competing theories about the necessary and sufficient conditions for blameworthiness. Some hold that an agent must meet a threshold of causal contribution to be liable to compensatory duties for wrongdoing. If such theories are correct, then perhaps the answer to (a) above is "no." But even if the answer to (a) is no, this doesn't undermine my argument for a negative answer to (c). My claim is not that state officials are immune from liability because ordinary citizens are substantively liable to bear costs of compensating victims of reasonable but unjust laws. My claim is rather that it would be unfair to hold state officials liable to defensive harm for enforcing reasonable but unjust laws when such laws are the unavoidable by-product of our collective and good-faith effort to live together on fair terms. My argument for a particular answer to (c) is independent of what one thinks about the answer to (a). Pointing to individual citizens' lack of causal contribution is thus not relevant.

The same point applies to the relationship between (b) and (c). The claim that state officials are not liable does not depend on the further idea that ordinary citizens are blameworthy. The two issues are even more clearly distinct. But since the point about citizens' lack of causal control applies most naturally to (a) and (b), it doesn't threaten what I want to say about (c).

What of the other issue—the fact that state officials are not conscripts, but rather make the voluntary choice to take up their

---

35. As compared to (c), there is a fairly developed recent literature on questions (a) and (b). See, for example, Lawford-Smith, *Not in Their Name*; Pasternak, *Responsible Citizens*; Stilz, "Are Citizens Culpable."

role? This might seem more clearly relevant to (c). If A volunteers for a role that she can foresee involves the risk of violating people's rights, how can she claim it's unfair to hold her liable to harm if that risk eventuates? If she doesn't want to be exposed to such a risk, she needn't volunteer. The general principle might be something like this:

> *Voluntary Assumption*: If you volunteer to do something morally risky, it's not unfair to hold you liable if the moral risk eventuates.

This principle, though sound in some contexts, is not generally true. The principle works well in cases where the morally risky activity is optional, and being voluntarily pursued as part of someone's personal plans or projects. But the principle is much less plausible when the morally risky activity is one that is both morally required, and not done to advance any particular person or group's plans or projects. In the former cases, it seems appropriate to tell the agent, "You didn't have to do this, you undertook the risky activity to advance your own projects, and thus it's only fair that you, rather than others, bear the costs for any errors that you make." But this statement is inapt in the latter set of cases. Even if it's true that a specific person didn't have to take up the role, it still had to be taken up by someone. Put differently: taking up the role is individually optional, but not collectively optional.[36] This matters when considering whether it's fair to hold a given individual liable for the errors that someone is going to have to make. If we, as a functioning political community, require various roles to be occupied that involve the risk of imposing unjust laws, the fact these roles are voluntarily taken up does not suffice to turn the resulting errors into private optional choices for which the office-holders are uniquely liable. The errors remain a collective burden.

---

36. There's a structural analogy here to what G. A. Cohen says about collective unfreedom. See Cohen, "Structure of Proletarian Unfreedom."

Conclusion

The puzzle of legitimate injustice revolves around three claims:

1) "Justice is the first virtue of social institutions, as truth is of systems of thought. A theory however elegant and economical must be rejected or revised if it is untrue; likewise laws and institutions no matter how efficient and well-arranged must be reformed or abolished if they are unjust."[37]

2) Some ordinary laws in liberal democratic societies are unjust.

3) Many of these laws can be legitimate: that is, state officials act permissibly in enforcing these laws and they have rights against harmful interference while enforcing them.

Though many of us are inclined to accept all three claims, affirming all three is at least prima facie puzzling. I have argued, however, that we can affirm all three claims. The burden of unjust law is a permanent feature of any realistic, free society. Justice requires that we share in the responsibility for this burden—we cannot outsource liability for these errors to officials who act within the limits of their democratically authorized roles. Sharing responsibility for our political errors also requires state officials to exclude their own first-order judgments about the (in)justice of reasonable legislative decisions, and so it follows that state officials can often act permissibly in enforcing unjust laws. But the explanation of this fact is still rooted in the priority of justice itself.

Although the account of legitimate injustice defended in this final chapter differs from the accounts canvassed in the earlier chapters, the arguments in this chapter do not require wholesale rejection of some of those other pictures of political morality. In particular, this chapter does not offer a general theory of political legitimacy. In that sense, the arguments in this chapter allow for the possibility that Kantian, or instrumental, or non-instrumental

37. Rawls, *Theory of Justice*, 3.

egalitarian arguments might be required for a complete theory of political legitimacy. I take no position on that here. I have only argued that these different pictures of political legitimacy cannot, on their own, adequately explain the phenomenon of legitimate injustice.

But the claims advanced in this chapter do have some important implications for more general theories of political morality. First, the best way to explain legitimate injustice is by an appeal to justice itself. We should thus be skeptical of any picture of political morality whereby the legitimacy of democratic decisions is not explained by such an appeal. Without an appeal to justice itself, it remains mysterious how government officials could possess protected claim rights to permissibly impose unjust laws.

Second, we cannot explain legitimate injustice without an appeal to some notion of political disagreement being reasonable. If disagreements about politics were always caused by prejudice, irrationality, or self-interest, I doubt there would be a compelling explanation of legitimate injustice. If we are—as I think we should be—inclined to accept legitimate injustice as a real and pervasive feature of political life, then I think we have good reasons to reject theories of political morality that deny or minimize significance of reasonable disagreement about politics.

At the outset of the book I said that contemporary political philosophy has been dominated by two questions: "Who gets what?"; and "Says who?" Theories of justice purport to answer the former question, and theories of political legitimacy aim to answer the latter. But because the answers to these two questions have often been pursued in isolation, there appears to be a deep tension at the heart of political morality. What happens when the answers to these questions pull us in opposite directions?

A general lesson to be drawn is that it is a mistake to pursue theories of justice and political legitimacy in isolation. There cannot be a successful account of political legitimacy that is indifferent to matters of justice. And any theory of justice that is unconcerned with political legitimacy is radically incomplete. Theories of justice should tell us how to share fairly in the burdens and benefits of our cooperative life. Making mistakes about laws and policies is one of the unavoidable burdens of our cooperative life, and so theories of justice must have something to say about this burden. And this has clear implications for our understanding of the nature and scope of political legitimacy.

BIBLIOGRAPHY

Applbaum, Arthur Isak. *Legitimacy: The Right to Rule in a Wanton World*. Harvard University Press, 2019.

Arneson, Richard J. "Defending the Purely Instrumental Account of Democratic Legitimacy." *Journal of Political Philosophy* 11, no. 1 (2003): 122–32.

Bolinger, Renée Jorgensen. "The Moral Grounds of Reasonably Mistaken Self-Defense." *Philosophy and Phenomenological Research* 103, no. 1 (2021): 140–56.

Brennan, Jason. "The Right to a Competent Electorate." *The Philosophical Quarterly* 61, no. 245 (2011): 700–724.

Brennan, Jason. *When All Else Fails: The Ethics of Resistance to State Injustice*. Princeton University Press, 2018.

Buchanan, Allen. *Justice, Legitimacy, and Self-Determination: Moral Foundations for International Law*. Oxford University Press, 2003.

Christiano, Thomas. *The Constitution of Equality*. Oxford University Press, 2008.

Cohen, G. A. "Fairness and Legitimacy in Justice, and: Does Option Luck Every Preserve Justice?" In *Hillel Steiner and the Anatomy of Justice: Themes and Challenges*, edited by Stephen de Wijze, Matthew Kramer, and Ian Carter. Routledge, 2009.

Cohen, G. A. *Rescuing Justice and Equality*. Harvard University Press, 2008.

Cohen, G. A. "The Structure of Proletarian Unfreedom." *Philosophy & Public Affairs* 12, no. 1 (1983): 3–33.

Davis, Ryan. "Justice: Do It." Unpublished manuscript.

Delmas, Candice. *A Duty to Resist: When Disobedience Should be Uncivil*. Oxford University Press, 2018.

Estlund, David. *Democratic Authority: A Philosophical Framework*. Princeton University Press, 2008

Ferzan, Kimberly Kessler. "Culpable Aggression: The Basis for Moral Liability to Defensive Killing." *Ohio State Journal of Criminal Law* 9, no. 2 (2012): 669–97.

Gaus, Gerald. *The Order of Public Reason: A Theory of Freedom and Morality in a Diverse and Bounded World*. Cambridge University Press, 2011.

Hamlin, Alan, and Zofia Stemplowska. "Theory, Ideal Theory, and the Theory of Ideals." *Political Studies Review* 10, no. 1 (2012): 48–62.

Hume, David. "Of the Original Contract." In David Hume, *Political Essays*, edited by Knud Haakonssen. Cambridge University Press, 1994.

Kant, Immanuel. *The Metaphysics of Morals*, edited and translated by Mary Gregor. Cambridge University Press, 1996.

Kant, Immanuel. "On the Common Saying: 'This May be True in Theory, but It Does Not Apply in Practice.'" In *Kant: Political Writings*, edited by Hans Reiss, translated by H. B. Nisbett. Cambridge University Press, 1991.

Kant, Immanuel. "Perpetual Peace: A Philosophical Sketch." In *Kant: Political Writings*, edited by Hans Reiss, translated by H. B. Nisbet. Cambridge University Press, 1991.

King, Loren. "The Federal Structure of a Republic of Reasons." *Political Theory* 33, no. 5 (2005): 629–53.

King, Martin Luther, Jr. *Letter from Birmingham Jail*. Penguin Classics, 2018.

Kolodny, Niko. "Being Under the Power of Others." In *Republicanism and the Future of Democracy*, edited by Yiftah Elazar and Geneviève Rousselière. Cambridge University Press, 2019.

Kolodny, Niko. *The Pecking Order: Social Hierarchy as a Philosophical Problem*. Harvard University Press, 2023.

Kolodny, Niko. "Rule Over None II: Social Equality and the Justification of Democracy." *Philosophy & Public Affairs* 42, no. 4 (2014): 287–336.

Landa, Dimitri, and Ryan Pevnick. *Representative Democracy: A Justification*. Oxford University Press, 2025.

Landemore, Hélène. *Democratic Reason: Politics, Collective Intelligence, and the Rule of the Many*. Princeton University Press, 2013.

Larmore, Charles. *What Is Political Philosophy?* Princeton University Press, 2020.

Lawford-Smith, Holly. *Not in Their Name: Are Citizens Culpable for Their States' Actions?* Oxford University Press, 2019.

Leonhardt, David. "Biden's Modest Tax Plan." *The New York Times*, May 4, 2021. https://www.nytimes.com/2021/05/04/briefing/biden-tax-plan-wealthy.html (accessed May 21, 2025).

Liberto, Hallie. "The Moral Specification of Rights: A Restricted Account." *Law and Philosophy* 33, no. 2 (2014): 175–206.

McConnell, Terrance. "Moral Dilemmas." In *The Stanford Encyclopedia of Philosophy*, Fall 2018 edition, edited by Edward N. Zalta. https://plato.stanford.edu/archives/fall2018/entries/moral-dilemmas/ (accessed May 21, 2025).

McMahan, Jeff. "The Basis of Moral Liability to Defensive Killing." *Philosophical Issues* 15, no. 1 (2005): 386–405.

McMahan, Jeff. *Killing in War*. Oxford University Press, 2009.

Nozick, Robert. *Anarchy, State, and Utopia*. Basic Books, 1974.

Oberdiek, John. "Specifying Rights Out of Necessity." *Oxford Journal of Legal Studies* 28, no. 1 (2008): 127–46.

Øverland, Gerhard, and Christian Barry. "Do Democratic Societies Have a Right to Do Wrong?" *Journal of Social Philosophy* 42, no. 2 (2011): 111–31.

Pallikkathayil, Japa. "Deriving Morality from Politics: Rethinking the Formula of Humanity." *Ethics* 121, no. 1 (2010): 116–47.

Pallikkathayil, Japa. "Neither Perfectionism nor Political Liberalism." *Philosophy & Public Affairs* 44, no. 3 (2016): 171–96.

Parfit, Derek. *On What Matters, Volume 1*. Oxford University Press, 2011.

Parry, Jonathan. "Authority and Harm." In *Oxford Studies in Political Philosophy, Volume 3*, edited by David Sobel, Peter Vallentyne, and Steven Wall. Oxford University Press, 2017.

Pasternak, Avia. *No Justice, No Peace: The Ethics of Violent Protests*. Oxford University Press, 2025.

Pasternak, Avia. *Responsible Citizens, Irresponsible States: Should Citizens Pay for Their States' Wrongdoing?* Oxford University Press, 2021.

Pettit, Philip. "Justice: Social and Political." In *Oxford Studies in Political Philosophy, Volume 1*, edited by David Sobel, Peter Vallentyne, and Steven Wall. Oxford University Press, 2015.

Quong, Jonathan. "Legitimate Injustice: A Response to Wellman." *Journal of Political Philosophy* 31, no. 2 (2023): 222–32.

Quong, Jonathan. *Liberalism without Perfection*. Oxford University Press, 2011.

Quong, Jonathan. *The Morality of Defensive Force*. Oxford University Press, 2020.

Rawls, John. *Justice as Fairness: A Restatement*. Harvard University Press, 2001.

Rawls, John. *Political Liberalism*. Paperback edition. Columbia University Press, 1996.

Rawls, John. *A Theory of Justice*. Revised edition. Oxford University Press, 1999.

Raz, Joseph. *The Authority of Law: Essays on Law and Morality*. Oxford University Press, 1979.

Raz, Joseph. *Engaging Reason: On the Theory of Value and Action*. Oxford University Press, 1999.

Raz, Joseph. *The Morality of Freedom*. Oxford University Press, 1986.

Ripstein, Arthur. "Authority and Coercion." *Philosophy & Public Affairs* 32, no. 1 (2004): 2–35.

Ripstein, Arthur. *Force and Freedom: Kant's Legal and Political Philosophy*. Harvard University Press, 2009.

Rossi, Enzo, and Matt Sleat. "Realism in Normative Political Theory." *Philosophy Compass* 9, no. 10 (2014): 689–701.

Sanders, Bernie. "Bernie Sanders on Economic Inequality." https://web.archive.org/web/20210615133239/https://feelthebern.org/bernie-sanders-on-economic-inequality/ (accessed June 21, 2025)

Scanlon, T. M. *What We Owe to Each Other*. Harvard University Press, 1998.

Schouten, Gina. *The Anatomy of Justice: On the Shape, Substance, and Power of Liberal Egalitarianism.* Oxford University Press, 2024.

Shelby, Tommie. *Dark Ghettos: Injustice, Dissent, and Reform.* Harvard University Press, 2016.

Shiffrin, Seana Valentine. *Democratic Law.* Oxford University Press, 2021.

Simmons, A. John. "Justification and Legitimacy." *Ethics* 109, no. 4 (1999): 739–71.

Sinclair, Thomas. "The Power of Public Positions." In *Oxford Studies in Political Philosophy, Volume 4,* edited by David Sobel, Peter Vallentyne, and Steven Wall. Oxford University Press, 2018.

Steiner, Hillel. *An Essay on Rights.* Blackwell, 1994.

Stemplowska, Zofia, and Adam Swift. "Dethroning Democratic Legitimacy." In *Oxford Studies in Political Philosophy, Volume 4,* edited by David Sobel, Peter Vallentyne, and Steven Wall. Oxford University Press, 2018.

Stilz, Anna. "Are Citizens Culpable for State Action?" *Politics, Philosophy, & Economics* 22, no. 4 (2023): 381–406.

Stilz, Anna. *Liberal Loyalty: Freedom, Obligation, and the State.* Princeton University Press, 2009.

Stoll, Ira. "Here's How Biden's Proposed Tax Increases Will Affect You." *Reason: Free Minds and Free Markets,* March 29, 2021. https://reason.com/2021/03/29/heres-how-bidens-proposed-tax-increases-will-affect-you/# (accessed May 21, 2025).

Stone, Rebecca. "Putting Freedom of Contract in Its Place." *Journal of Legal Analysis* 16, no. 1 (2024): 94–119.

Valentini, Laura. "Ideal vs. Non-ideal Theory: A Conceptual Map." *Philosophy Compass* 7, no. 9 (2012): 654–64.

Valentini, Laura. "Justice, Disagreement, and Democracy." *British Journal of Political Science* 43, no. 1 (2013): 177–99.

van der Vossen, Bas. "Consent to Unjust Institutions." *Legal Theory* 27, no. 3 (2021): 236–51.

Viehoff, Daniel. "Democratic Equality and Political Authority." *Philosophy & Public Affairs* 42, no. 4 (2014): 337–75.

Viehoff, Daniel. "Legitimate Injustice and Acting for Others." *Philosophy & Public Affairs* 50, no. 3 (2022): 301–74.

Viehoff, Daniel. "Power and Equality." In *Oxford Studies in Political Philosophy, Volume 5,* edited by David Sobel, Peter Vallentyne, and Steven Wall. Oxford University Press, 2019: 1–38.

Weinrib, Ernest. *The Idea of Private Law.* Revised edition. Oxford University Press, 2012.

Wellman, Christopher H. "Liberalism, Samaritanism, and Political Legitimacy." *Philosophy & Public Affairs* 25, no. 3 (1996): 211–37.

Wellman, Christopher H. "The Space Between Justice and Legitimacy." *Journal of Political Philosophy* 31, no. 1 (2023): 3–23.

Wellman, Christopher H., and A. John Simmons. *Is There a Duty to Obey the Law?* Cambridge University Press, 2005.

Wolff, Jonathan. *An Introduction to Political Philosophy.* Revised edition. Oxford University Press, 2006.

INDEX